MW01243695

how to help and encourage your child

who has been diagnosed with
bipolar disorder, major depression, or
borderline personality disorder

speaking to the heart of your hurting child

kimberly griffin

This is my heart's cry:

Remember your child is in pain.
It is heartbreaking to see our children hurt. And although
their behaviors can be unusual or dark or confusing,
if we can remember that our babies are in pain, then
we can respond with compassion and patience.

Pour into the relationship.
Our relationships with our children are vital. It is essential
to work at maintaining, possibly mending, and continually
building up our relationships with our children if we seek
a future of warmth and health and intimacy.

Pour out love.
Lovelovelove. Our children need to know that they
are loved unconditionally. Let your love flow over them,
seeping into every cell and fiber of their being, at all times.
Hope and healing begin here.

Hold on to hope. It's the only way.

TABLE OF CONTENTS

PREFACE

If you are loving a child who has received one of these diagnoses, my heart goes out to you. It is an extremely delicate, excruciatingly painful place to be. And we need help.

My name is Kimberly, and I am a mom. I am not a doctor, a nurse, a psychologist, or a social worker. There are no titles or letters that follow my name. I'm just one hurting momma trying to spread love, encourage healing, hope, and help to anybody else along the way.

I love being a mom. I love my children with all my heart. I love all children — and that's why I'm writing. I live and love in this painful place, too. I am simply sharing what experience, research, and perseverance have taught me. In order for us to be able to help our loved ones, we need to have strong relationships with them. We must be able to touch them deeply, and to *speak the language that their hurting hearts can hear.*

Perhaps you are in shock over recent behavioral changes in your child. Many of us struggle and wonder and ache for years before our children receive an accurate diagnosis. We hurt alongside our babies. And while it may be hard to accept the truth of a such a diagnosis, for our children's sake, we must. *Their healing and well-being are rooted in our support and care.* (Toward the end of this book, I include a few coping suggestions for parents.) Please note that this is not an informational piece about bipolar disorder, major depression, or borderline personality disorder, although recommendations will be given. I have found this to be a very lonely and painful path, and therefore I hope to lend some companionship for the journey. This work is intended to provide support and practical, specific help for parents in living with, loving, helping, and encouraging a child of any age who has been diagnosed with a challenging and painful illness.

As a teen, our daughter was diagnosed with anxiety and depression, later borderline personality disorder, and after years of pain, the shattering tragedy of the death of her daughter, and further crises, a lengthier hospitalization followed by intensive psychological testing added bipolar disorder with psychotic features and post-traumatic stress disorder to her diagnosis.

I write with a spirit of tender urgency. I write because there is no time to waste. Many of us in this circumstance face the pain of suicidality. Our daughter has made three attempts at ending her own life, and the third one nearly took her from us. I am sharing ways we have been loving her back to life.

CHAPTER ONE

Thoughts from this Mother's Heart

I poured out my heart on the opening page, but the message bears repeating … to enable ourselves to truly help our loved ones, we must open our eyes and keep them fixed on this premise: our children are in pain. With this in view, we respond to their behaviors, however unusual, dark, or confusing, with compassion and patience. We create an environment of warmth and health and intimacy where love overflows, our children feel heard, and hope and healing take root. Breathe deeply; keep reading.

So how do we help and encourage our hurting children? How do we respond to them in a manner that will ensure they feel loved and accepted, and ultimately lead them to healthy, safe, and hopeful living?

Respond with Love

Remembering that our children are in pain will help us as we allow compassion to fill our hearts before we respond to our children's outcries or behaviors. *lovelovelove*

Build up the Relationships

In order to reach the hearts and minds of our children, we need to build up our relationships. Strong, healthy relationships with our children grant us the most favorable foundation for encouraging healthy thinking and decision making, soothing emotions, and living with promise and hope. Sometimes this can be challenging because the pain our children suffer causes them to react inconsistently. A friend calls this the "grab and push-away syndrome" — at times our children ache for us, reach for us, and drink in what we offer; in other instances, they push us away. Their hurting souls have special needs that require the gentle touch that comes from a deep place of understanding and connection. And even as we endeavor to better understand them, we need to be speaking from a heart of compassion, with love flavoring our speech. This is true for all of our children, but for our kids with these disorders, it is imperative. Everything I share in these pages is intended to help you develop this healing connection.

Beyond love, I believe the primary building blocks of good relationships include empathy and communication. These are the arteries that carry our love to our children; this is the heart of my message. Therefore, attention is given to this in the Language that Loves, Lifts, and Heals (Chapter Five). For individuals living with bipolar disorder, major depression, or borderline personality disorder, communication is especially important. It is interesting to learn that often just the smallest revisions in our language, in the way we phrase things, may further nurture relationships and promote healthier brain processing.

An essential part of communication is listening. Listen with your ears, your eyes, your whole heart. Pay attention to more than their words. Observe body language, tones, behaviors. The expression that resounds within me is, we "enter in." We fully engage — leaning in, placing ourselves where they are, experiencing what they are feeling — our hearts hearing and beating with theirs.

While so much more can be said about building relationships, I will simply add here that it is helpful and healing if we can stay flexible, open, positive, and — especially important — if we can cultivate an ongoing spirit of forgiveness and hope.

Touch the heart of their emotions first

It is true for all of us that during times of intense emotions, it's hard to think clearly, make decisions, or be certain of what to do next. Our children with these diagnoses find emotions to be even more overwhelming than most of us can imagine. The very nature of these disorders entails emotion overload.

When our children are in emotional distress …

>*it doesn't matter what we think about the trigger,*

>*it doesn't matter how we think a problem might be solved,*

>*it doesn't matter what our feelings are,*

>*and there is no right or wrong about feelings.*

What matters are our responses to our children; particularly how we interact with them during times of emotional distress. So BEFORE we help them handle issues, problems, or consequences, we must appropriately respond with love and concern to their emotions. *This is how they feel heard.*

In the first two chapters, I share a few initial thoughts pertaining to our roles, our care, and our efforts. Chapter Three briefly presents important, informative building blocks for the remainder of the book. This is followed by messages from hurting hearts graciously shared by a few special and brave individuals. Chapter Five highlights caring communication that will connect our hearts, strengthen relationships, and help children reset their brains toward healthier processing. Next, I offer book reviews that matter, and recommend excellent books that fully develop those concepts. If you are overwhelmed, in crisis, or panicking over what to do, it may be hard to sit down with a stack of large books and begin studying. Therefore, it is my great hope to facilitate immediate, appropriate action toward deeper relationships, better mental health, and improved behavior by pointing you directly to sources of real, meaningful help. After that, I outline several other beneficial ideas, discuss suicide prevention, share coping strategies, and finally, I provide a list of outstanding resources — all intended to strengthen and support us as we strive to speak to the hearts of our hurting children.

CHAPTER TWO

Finding Our Compass

In spite of our own shock or pain, we are the parents, and if we are invested in our children and desire to do all that we can to help them, then we have our work to do. For the most part, our efforts will fall into two categories: Our Immediate Work and Our Ongoing Work. Our Immediate Work deals with acceptance, managing the basics, and discovering help and resources. Our Ongoing Work involves many aspects of parenting that take on different forms when we are living with a challenging diagnosis. Further direction and practical suggestions are forthcoming in later chapters. Perhaps this preview can help you organize your thoughts.

Our Immediate Work

Acceptance

One of the first things we must do is accept the diagnosis. Certainly, if you question it, pursue additional professional opinions. And you may wish to ask for more intensive psychological testing, if your son or daughter is willing. But once the truth of a diagnosis is revealed, the best way forward is to accept it. Naturally, this is upsetting for any parent! It may require extra effort on our part to accept, cope, and gain strength to be able to best support our children. For now, I encourage you to open up your hearts, be brave, step outside of your comfort zone, get past the stigma, help fight the stigma by acknowledging, becoming educated, and seeking help. It is from a place of acceptance that we can begin to learn and grow and become the advocates and personal life coaches that our children desperately require. Allow me to repeat: their healing and well-being are rooted in our support and care.

Look at the Whole Package

Lessons we've acquired on this painful journey reflect that healing and better mental health are nourished by at least six critical components: the basics (nutrition, sleep, exercise), medication, good counseling, something productive for a loved one to do, a safe place to live, and the presence of loving, caring, supportive people. While we may not be in control of this, we must understand the importance of these necessary elements. It is crucial that we do all we can to ensure the basics of good health are in place.

Seeking Care

Finally, we might assist our children in the search for good counseling, locating support groups and/or reassuring individuals with some experience in this realm, and finding books and websites that can enlighten our families on this journey. (Tips regarding medication and finding a counselor are offered in the chapter on coaching life.) Depending upon the mental state, age, or willingness of a child, the efforts we make may vary, but we can offer to help — "May I make an appointment for you?" "Would you like a ride to your appointment?" — or simply offer emotional support and encouragement as they step into mental health care.

Once we find ourselves in a place of acceptance, have done our best to establish the basics, and have tracked down some good care for our children, we can focus on our Ongoing Work …

Our Ongoing Work

Study

Spend time reading and learning about the diagnosed condition(s).

You may already know by now that it is very common for people who have one diagnosis to also have a second diagnosis or disorder. For example, depression and anxiety often go hand in hand, as do alcoholism and depression. So, many of our children may be living with bipolar disorder, major depression, or borderline personality disorder *and* struggling with anxiety or some additional disorder, too. (The experts in the field refer to this as: comorbid, comorbidity, concomitant, or co-occurring.)

Study as much as possible, from symptoms to treatments. When we educate ourselves we can better understand our beloved children — the way their brains work, their emotional responses, and what we can do. The fact that you are reading this indicates you are already on this path. In addition to the books that will be referenced throughout and reviewed in Chapter Six, an organized list of useful books and websites appears in the Resources section. The more we know, the more we can help.

Fine-Tune Parenting Skills

Something you may not expect to hear (or read) is a plea to improve our parenting skills. Yet, here it is.

Even if we are already parenting with compassion, I invite you to be open and consider that we can always enhance our parenting abilities.

No matter the age of our children, we can purposefully enrich our relationships, refine our communication skills, and better reach our children's hearts. To this end, I highly recommend *Between Parent and Child* by Dr. Haim Ginott (more details given in Chapter Six). Offering practical teaching and clear guidance for parents to learn to shape behavior by reaching kids emotionally, his work provides the foundation for countless other parenting books, as well. His well-taught principles will benefit all families, and dovetail perfectly with the counsel given to meet the needs of our children with emotional disorders.

Parent Introspection

We might need to honestly examine and address our hearts and approaches, because *our* thoughts and opinions and feelings are not the primary concern when our children are in distress. This is where we check ourselves — Have we accepted the diagnosis? Are we learning more about it? What is our priority in the moment? Are we attentive? Are we open? Difficult as this may be, we must put our children and their emotions first. This means we should listen, and weigh carefully our responses. Trite platitudes disappoint. Knee-jerk reactions, yelling, lecturing, criticizing and the like will get us nowhere. They don't build relationships, and they don't build up our children. I recall a trying occasion when a family member intervened with a "tough love" approach that had disastrous emotional consequences, led to self-mutilation, put several relationships at risk, and further broke my broken heart. We need to be doing our work so we are not reacting from a place of confusion or frustration. Also, if you are unaccustomed to a deep connection and intimate conversation, you may find some of your child's thoughts to be very challenging. Prepare yourself the best you can to hear about sex, cutting, suicidal thoughts, etc. Listen to the *pain* behind what they are sharing. Maintain an attitude of love that wants to help. Be gentle. This is delicate. Our words, our behaviors, and our reactions need to be focused on our hurting children. This doesn't mean we lift rules or eliminate consequences — but we work through emotions and relate in a different manner to bring change (more in Chapter Five). And we must be strong in order to help our children, so if we need to address our own issues, we might pursue our own counseling, seek support groups, or utilize other options shared later in the chapter on coping. (Their hearts matter, yet our hearts matter, too.)

Persevere

Other elements of our Ongoing Work, described in subsequent chapters in this small book, include: communicating, encouraging, and coaching our children. We continue to pursue the help our children need while studying, doing our best to maintain the basics, as well as working on ourselves to cultivate measures for coping and persevering. We cannot do all of this at once, but we can look at our own family, and our own child's needs, and determine to take certain small steps toward building health and strength. And we may be doing this for a long time. It may seem challenging, but we must keep doing our work, pouring out love, and maintaining a spirit of hope.

CHAPTER THREE

Prelude to the Rest

Before we proceed, just a few introductory words regarding the books, the brain, heart, and the healing balm of speech will better equip us to receive and absorb the content.

A word about the books:

After reading a myriad of books on mental illness, I found myself drawn to a few that really spoke to the way my heart responded to my children. Not all the books in this category emphasize the things we can be doing at home that can nurture health and healing. Yet we are on the front lines! We are the ones watching our children suffer every single day! We are the ones who love so deeply and care so much! We are the ones fully invested in their lives!

We need help.

Many fine sources for information are available, in fact, SO many!! My hope is to cut through the vast number of books and resources and direct you to the best of the many that I have studied. I believe the extraordinary books referenced throughout and reviewed in Chapter Six provide invaluable wisdom, comprehensive knowledge, and empathetic guidance for loving and encouraging all hurting souls.

A word about the brain:

It seems sensible to have a teeny bit of background information on the brain. It is important for us to understand that the brains of individuals with bipolar disorder, major depression, or borderline personality disorder are wired differently. I am going to sum this up in a frighteningly simplistic manner (any professional might gasp), but this booklet is intended to provide immediate, accessible help to parents. Primitive as this may be, it has been my way of interpreting the physiology so I could move on to the critical work of breathing life and love into a hurting girl.

In the brain we have the "thinking part," located in the neocortex, and we have the "emotion part," called the amygdala. As I visualize it, the brains of individuals with such disorders tend to "think" more with their amygdala, or the emotion center. Importantly, impaired amygdala function is indicated in the brains of individuals with certain mental disorders (Wikipedia. The National Institute of Mental Health, NIMH, documents this, too; their website is very informative.) Many of the books on mental illness discuss brain function at length and attempt to explain these complex processes to laypeople like me. The book that I believe describes it best is not specific to mental illness, yet I cannot imagine a better portrayal of the way the brain deals with emotions than Daniel Goleman's *Emotional Intelligence*. Just the title of his second chapter, "Anatomy of an Emotional Hijacking," speaks volumes. Depth of knowledge and succinct communication are evident as Goleman expounds "the neural takeover" in the (aptly named) hijacking (Goleman, 1995, p. 14). His metaphors, quite frankly, *land it*.

Emotions are human and natural. As Goleman illustrates brain response to stimuli from the senses, he makes it clear that we need both the rational *and* the emotional elements to work in balance in a healthy mind (Goleman, 1995, p. 26). Essentially, a tiny little synapse in the brain allows the amygdala the opportunity to react before the neocortex does. Useful in fight or flight urgency, this can otherwise lead to emotional flooding and consequent impulsive or irrational behaviors if not checked by the prefrontal cortex. The complex cortical center requires a bit more time, but ultimately, all circuits should operate together in appropriate processing (p. 25). If this is the design of the human brain's "architecture" (p. 16), then when we picture a brain with a mental disorder or chemical imbalance, it magnifies the impact of constant overwhelming emotions and "emotional emergencies" (p. 17). And that brings us back to our hurting children.

I have limited this discourse to the area in which we, as parents, can play a part in helping to calm the brain and foster healthier thinking processes. Along the path, we have been counseled about the importance of acknowledging and accepting emotions as key to emotional health. Counselors and books taught me that the elementary process of *naming* our emotions moves brain activity from the amygdala to the prefrontal cortex, which generates a calmer emotional function and initiates cortical activity (e.g. Goleman, 1995, p. 47).

In your studies, you can delve further into the medical reports on these intricate neurological processes. I'm sharing this abbreviated perspective as a base from which to say that our efforts of support and communication can complement the therapies used in counseling and assist us in gently guiding our children toward healthier ways of thinking and behaving.

A word about heart:

I frequently refer to the "heart" involved in caring for our loved ones. While the term takes on several familiar meanings, occasionally it expresses something greater. As our hearts are central and vital to wholeness and health in our bodies, heart, in this sense, also embraces love, empathy, and ultimate caring. Heart breeds courage and strength. Connoting our intentional choice to help, it envelops with a spirit of generosity, kindness, forgiveness, and patience. Heart lovingly opens up compassionate spaces for nurturing connection; it is accepting, deepening, and energizing.

Heart lovingly opens up compassionate spaces for nurturing connection; it is accepting, deepening, and energizing.

A word about our words:

If we are pouring out love and remembering that our children are in pain, we can engage with earnestness to help. For our kids with these diagnoses, feeling the love is all the more critical. Their aching souls are incredibly sensitive. We convey love in numerous ways, and our hurting children may need even more expressions of our love.

Relational, emotionally sensitive parenting invites us to connect and communicate well. Our tones and attitudes deliver strong messages. We must keep our mouths aligned with our hearts. *Our words matter.* They can wound or heal. They can dig down deep into souls. They can echo for ages.

Our loving responses are particularly important when our children are in distress. That is why our first calling is to touch the heart of their emotions. Responding with empathy and compassion, we affirm, or validate, those feelings. And this affirmation is the threshold to their hearts, because this is where we begin speaking the language their hearts can hear.

Validation is the language that loves, lifts, and heals.

References

Amygdala. (n.d.) In Wikipedia. Retrieved August 23, 2016 from http.//en.wikipedia/ Amygdala.

"Brain Basics" (n.d.), National Institute of Mental Health. Retrieved August 23, 2016 from www.nimh.nih.gov.

"Emotion Regulation Circuit Weakened in Borderline Personality Disorder" (October 2, 2008), National Institute of Mental Health. Retrieved August 23, 2016 from www.nimh.nih.gov.

Goleman, Daniel. *Emotional Intelligence.* New York: Bantam Books, 1995. Print.

CHAPTER FOUR

Voices from the Valley

To My Mental Illnesses
I wish we had never met,
you and I.
You taught me how to hate,
and it's you I despise.
Your claws puncture my throat
as I try to speak my mind.
When I hide, you seek
and you always find.
You're the only one that binds me
in a way I can't untie.
Fear and shame are all I have
if you are by my side.
I try to leave my house
but it's a maze when you're inside.
You trip me on the stairs,
you fill my head with lies.
The more I live with you,
the more I want to die.
The more I fight with you,
the less I want to try.
You've made me blind
throwing tears into my eyes
but I guess it doesn't matter
because there is no end in sight;
you've torn off my wings
and I've forgotten how to fly.

– *The Author's Daughter*

As we seek to touch the hearts of our children with healing words and love, it is important to not only remember they are in pain, but to attempt to understand their pain. Perhaps you have not truly asked; perhaps you have not truly listened; perhaps your loved one cannot or will not express himself or herself. So I have reached out to my daughter for assistance. In her journey toward well-being, she and another woman created a Facebook group, called Shameless, dedicated to ending stigma and providing a safe place for individuals with mental illnesses to share. Within days, literally hundreds of hurting people had joined. Love, camaraderie, and creativity pour into and throughout this community.

Several vulnerable and brave individuals from the Shameless family were willing to share with me, in hopes of helping others. These beautiful hearts open up about the pain and darkness to enable loved ones to better understand the depths. I am touched and honored to have connected with them. Please, hear their voices.

What they wish people knew about their diagnosed conditions:

> "Sometimes it's like a trap. I'll be great for so long then randomly, I'll get down about something and it will be ridiculously hard to get back up. Sometimes the sadness affects my health. My stomach, my head, etc. Being alone is a blessing, but it is a huge curse too. I can go from thinking about one thing, down a rabbit trail, to feeling insanely sad and upset within 30 seconds. Find something to distract me and bring me back up."

> *Jenna, age 22, diagnosed with situational depression/ suicidality*

> "I AM NOT bipolar. I HAVE bipolar disorder. My illnesses do not define me."

> *Grace, age 25, diagnosed with depression, bipolar disorder, PTSD*

"Being bipolar does not just mean I'm an unpredictable basket case.

Having anxiety doesn't mean I'm afraid of everything.

Panic attacks are SCARY.

The same illness can look completely different on two different people. I often feel at odds with myself … There's me and there's the illness and we're battling for the controls. Medication gives me the upper hand MOST of the time.

I wish people talked about antepartum depression. Being depressed while you're pregnant is SO alienating. Being pregnant was arguably the worst 9 months of my life. I was anxious. I was suicidal. I took care of myself only for the baby. I missed a week of work because of rolling panic attacks. I eventually lost my job. I lived in a basement. I didn't have a car. My friends disappeared. On the rare occasion I saw anyone I had to put on this ridiculous act. My mom and my mother-in-law both had fertility issues so I was constantly reminded how BLESSED I was. I didn't feel blessed. I felt cursed, unimportant, forsaken, forgotten. I existed only to have this baby. I disappeared."

Cassidy, age 29, diagnosed with bipolar, general anxiety disorder, panic disorder, PTSD, antepartum/postpartum depression

"Many of us have been dealing with our various disorders since puberty or before. And the majority of us did so unmedicated. I wish people knew what a struggle it is to go through such an overwhelming time of your life while your mind is also fighting you. And that's what it feels like, at least that's what it felt like for me. Your brain is in constant battle. The majority of your brain is your disorder, the emotions and decision making. But there is a small part of your brain- way back in the back- that can still think logically about what you're thinking/feeling/doing. But that's all it can do. You know what you're doing is illogical. That your actions aren't you. That your emotions are not proportional to the trigger. But you can't do anything about it.

That is what was scariest for me. I didn't know what was happening, what was going on, why I was thinking and feeling the things I was. I think people need to know that, especially as an undiagnosed teen, we're going through our own horror story. Being trapped in our own minds [yet] with enough consciousness to know what's happening.

Please know that a diagnosis, while very helpful, is just words. It doesn't change the battle …"

J.B., age 25, diagnosed with rapid-cycling bipolar disorder, dependent personality disorder, general anxiety disorder

Things people have said during times of distress that were unhelpful or hurtful:

"Stop making everything a big deal."

"Just don't think about it."

"Think of something else …"

"Go out and do something fun."

"Maybe if you just did …"

"Maybe if you weren't …"

"You just want attention."

"You should pray about it."

"I don't know what you want ME to do!"

"I have been through hard things, too. You need to recognize that you have a lot to be grateful for …"

"Two years from now, you'll look back and feel silly for (insert emotional problem here) …"

"You are killing your parents."

This brief narrative explains: "I used to self-harm, pretty heavily, and people would say that anyone that did that was obviously just doing it for attention. I thought that was odd because I went through great lengths to make sure no one found out … When I was hospitalized … one of my friends went around telling people I just wanted attention. One of my exes said I was pathetic and just wanted people to feel sorry for me."

Heartbreaking themes of traps, cages, struggles, battles, and loneliness prevail. Sensitivity is critical; in these deep and dark valleys of pain the "Snap out of it" or "Pull yourself up by the bootstraps" mentality fails terribly. Common responses such as "Get a hold of yourself" or "Calm down" are not helpful, and can even induce the opposite effect. Often, loving, well-meaning people with good intentions inadvertently say things that can be damaging. In addition, Cassidy expressed that she has "… come to loathe the assumption that 'all teenagers are moody and will outgrow it.'" She wrote, "I heard this so often *I* was even surprised that I didn't outgrow it. I know it's a hard time, but cutting myself daily was not normal, and I didn't grow out of it. I recovered from it." Regrettably, some of the worst comments made are spoken by family members.

Things people have said during times of distress that were helpful or supportive:

"I would miss you so much, I don't know what I'd do without you."

"I won't leave you"

"Don't deny your feelings."

"Your pain is real."

"You're validated to feel the way you do."

"The storm around you is not greater than the one within you."

"Focus on blocks of time. Look to the next hour, if that's too much, do the next thirty minutes, if that's too much, do the next ten. All the way down to surviving the next second."

"Stop bull*****ing yourself. You're not OK. It's fine to not be OK. (Gotta love army-style bluntness.)"

"I love you."

Family revelation offered a healing message in one case: "Knowing that my whole family was also dealing with these issues gave me a better perspective to explain myself to them. My aunt was the first person in my family to ever say, 'It's OK if you need to take medication.' .... I don't feel like I'm hiding anymore."

What they WISH people would say (or do):

"I won't leave you."

"I'm going to see you through this."

"You wanna go _____ (hang out, for a hike, do something, etc.)?"

"I'll go see a counselor with you."

"Just [tell me] that it was okay … that WE would get through it … "

"I would love to hear: 'I'm so sorry, is there anything I can do?'"

"I understand, is this a time you need me, or need me to go in the other room?"

"I wish people would treat mental illness with the same respect as any other illness."

Cassidy further explained that the support of the word "we" helped: "That WE would get through it. It always felt like something I had to do alone and in secret. I know ultimately I am in charge of myself, but I don't have to do it alone. No one should have to." She spoke warmly of her supportive husband: "He also reminds me where I've been. When I have a bad day he'll say, ' … but it's not a bad week or month.'" J.B. poignantly remarked, "Please know that if I come to you and tell you something's wrong, I have trusted you- with something bigger than my heart."

Again, I so appreciate the help and heart in these disclosures. I hope hearing the voices of these courageous and generous individuals increases your understanding. Be encouraged; hope lies before us.

CHAPTER FIVE

The Language that Loves, Lifts, and Heals

With the voices from the valley still ringing within us, we arrive at the heart of this message, which is effective, healing, compassionate communication. Heartfelt communication, *validation* is important to all human beings, and indispensable to helping those who struggle with overpowering emotions. Validation is the language that will touch their hearts, soothe their minds, and lead to healing.

If we want to cultivate relationships that heal and bloom, we need to be a safe place for our loved ones. We begin with soft, loving, listening hearts; we *enter in* to their lives. Open and compassionate, we let them know we are listening; *we hear their hearts*. By acknowledging and understanding our children's emotions, we validate — speaking love and affirmations which anoint hurting souls with a cool, healing balm.

Validation was identified as a tool for helping individuals with emotional dysregulation and/or suicidality by Marsha Linehan, Ph.D. A professor, researcher, and clinician, Dr. Linehan also developed Dialectical Behavior Therapy (DBT), a vital treatment in the field. The National Alliance on Mental Illness (NAMI) honored Linehan with their 2015 Scientific Research Award, and in an interview posted on their website (October 5, 2015), Linehan described her experiences in providing treatment, and her discovery of the importance of integrating acceptance *with* change, plus a few other components, as the core of successful DBT.

Validation lies at the root of that acceptance.

In the article, Linehan explains that part of acceptance is being nonjudgmental, which can be challenging. It does not infer agreement with the behavior or thinking, however. Being nonjudgmental in a validating response simply acknowledges and accepts the other person's *feelings* about a situation.

Further investigation of her findings, presented in numerous books discussing the topic (see Chapter Six), reveals Linehan's six levels of validation. Beyond the scope of this piece, these elements are well-worth studying for deeper understanding. Linehan's invaluable work is referenced or quoted in all literature on validation or DBT that I have read. Her successes have profoundly influenced mental health care, and delivered help and hope to many.

So we tend to the emotions first. We touch heart to heart. We respond with love. We speak the language that loves, lifts, and heals.

And that's just what validation does. Understanding, absorbing, and implementing this salient concept will greatly impact our relationships and the mental health of our loved ones. In the following chapter, *Book Reviews that Matter*, I'll introduce you to excellent resources that will further equip us in learning and embracing this language of love and healing. Unconventional as it may be, to ease explanation, enhance comprehension, and offer convenience, sources referenced herein are noted in the scientific, in-text format — with page numbers — and will be documented at the chapter end as well as listed in the References section. All of the books referenced in this chapter will be reviewed in the next chapter. I hope to provide a brief explanation, then show you exactly where to go to continue your education. Far beyond citing sources, I am recommending the titles of vital books for our families.

Emotions are natural and spontaneous. As we love and encourage children who are flooded by emotions, we allow them to express themselves; we comfort them by validating, and as they acknowledge their feelings and absorb our validating love, brain activity is altered, shifting toward better cognitive functioning, thus improving mental health and behavior (Goleman, 1995, p. 47). Validation comes alongside and says "I hear you." Dr. Haim Ginott explains that assuring normalcy brings tremendous relief (Ginott, 2003, p. 21). Validating language builds a bond, creating an atmosphere of warmth and trust that provides comfort to a hurting person. Validation compassionately acknowledges and affirms a person's emotions.

*Validation compassionately acknowledges
and affirms a person's emotions.*

Empathy helps us enter in: "I'd be upset, too, if ... " "Of course you're sad! That's a lot to take ... " "Anybody would cry if ... " We all need empathy and validation. Compassion in action, validation helps us all feel normal and understood; it communicates love. And better than that, validation helps us feel *connected*.

Again, validation compassionately acknowledges and affirms a person's emotions. In *Overcoming Borderline Personality Disorder*, Valerie Porr, MA, refers to validation as an "art" (Porr, 2010, p. 130), dubbing it an "emotional language" (p. 134). In *The Power of Validation* by Karyn Hall, Ph.D., and Melissa H. Cook, LPC, the authors say we are accepting someone's "emotional experience" (Hall and Cook, 2012, p. 50). They emphasize acknowledging and accepting the "internal experience" and expressing its validity with understanding and empathy (p. 33). Emotions are real; emotions are neither right nor wrong; emotions are valid. I believe it is critical that we, as parents, reflect upon and remember to maintain perspective on their emotional or internal experiences as we respond to our emotionally distressed children. *Our children are in pain.*

According to the experts, in addition to soothing emotions (Porr, 2010, p. 132; Manning, 2011, p. 55), and building relationships, validation also creates a sense of identity and even self-confidence (Hall and Cook, 2012, pp. 30, 36). Additionally, Karyn Hall and Melissa Cook assert that validation provides an outlet for strong emotions (Hall and Cook, p. 19), concurring with Daniel Goleman that knowing, accepting, and experiencing our emotions help us learn how to cope with and manage them (Hall and Cook, pp. 50,53; Goleman, 1995, pp. 47–49). Goleman clearly states that awareness is the foundation of emotional control (Goleman, p. 47). Validation can help our children trust themselves! Incorporating validation into our communication can help us lead our children to self-reliance and resilience.

Interestingly, in their definitions, the professionals illustrate what validation *is* by underscoring what validation is *not* (for the following please refer to Hall and Cook, 2012, pp. 14–21; Porr, 2010, pp. 167–177; Manning, 2011, p. 59). Virtually every expert writing on this pertinent topic warns us that validation is …

> … not agreeing

> … not permissive

> … not fixing

> … not praise or compliments

> … not lying

> … not following a script

Fleshing that out just a minute degree, we recall that validation responds to our children's feelings, not to their behavior. As Dr. Linehan points out, it does not mean we agree with the thoughts or behavior; we are first affirming the emotion behind it (Linehan, 2015, www.nami.org). Validation is not permissive in that we still address behavior once emotions have been acknowledged and regulated (Hall and Cook, p. 15). Amongst the most challenging "nots" is the fact that validation is not "fixing," that is, we do not rush out to fix a problem or cover it up or try to make it better or try to change the emotions. This one can especially be hard if our children have truly put themselves in troublesome situations. Doubtless, at some point most of us have intervened where we could have guided. We leap in with solutions or logical ideas before emotions are settled, or before we give our darlings the chance to figure it out for themselves. Validation simply responds to emotions in a loving and accepting manner. Often *that* is the primary thing needed. Refraining from judgment, criticism, and dictatorial parenting, we accept and love. Regarding the praise and compliments, this one can be subtle, and even tricky. Astonishingly, praise can actually have the opposite effect, and invalidate! Valerie Porr explains praise may appear judgmental, leaving the impression that an outcome only matters if we approve (whoa!), and counsels us to remark on the *effort made* (Porr, p. 168). (Dr. Haim Ginott teaches this principle well in his second chapter, "The

Power of Words.") The distinction may seem so slight, but this enlightening lesson can help us strengthen our children, and build confidence — even if it might be a bit humbling for some of us! Validation responds with love to what someone is feeling.

Validation responds with love
to what someone is feeling.

Also, we don't lie when we validate. If our child fails an exam or loses a job, we don't tell him he did well! We validate his *emotions* about the problem — THEN the consequences can be discussed. Validation is not scripted; life is unpredictable; our circumstances vary; there is not a particular "word prescription" for us to employ. Our words must be honest, sincere, and come from the heart. We look for their truth, speak what we know is true (their feelings are true); so we validate the valid. Perhaps we have to ask questions to find the truth behind emotions, but validation responds with love to what someone is feeling. And this heart-language works through their hearts and minds, initiating appropriate thinking processes which can lead to positive discussions about behavior, consequences, and choices.

By now you may already be able to see how our words validate or invalidate as expressed by the voices from the valley. Their collective histories clearly depict both the absence of validation and what validation looks like. In one passage, for example, Cassidy shared a powerful message of being invalidated regarding her pregnancy. Compare other hurtful types of comments shared by the Shameless members ("Just don't think about it." "You just want attention.") with the helpful and supportive ones ("Your pain is real." It's OK not to be OK." "I love you."). The difference is palpable.

> "Validation. That's a big one. Just hearing that I was ALLOWED to feel the way I felt. My last therapist told me that. My husband is very supportive. He knows my illness is not based objectively on how well things are going."

> – Cassidy

"My depression is controlled really well with medication. But there are no meds to make me feel validated without someone telling me that I am."

– J.B.

Take *that* in.

We touch the heart of their emotions first. We pour out love to our hurting children through listening, through empathy, through our words. We may gently ask questions, like "How can I help?" Or we may hold them in our arms and feebly confess, "I wish I knew what to say. But I'm here." Validation helps our children feel heard. Validation saturates our relationships with heart. And *heart lovingly opens up compassionate spaces for nurturing connection; it is accepting, deepening, and energizing.*

This type of emotional communication comes naturally for some of us and weaves its way into parenting automatically. Some may find the concept of validation familiar, yet not be practicing it. However, if this is foreign to you, or if you recognize yourself in any of the less desirable messages shared previously, take heart; it is never too late. Take a deep breath, forgive yourself, and start fresh. It all begins with love. From here, we layer on understanding, compassion, and hope.

Please remember, I'm attempting to take a very remarkable concept, distill it, and present it briefly for quick, accessible support. Pursuing validation to the fullest extent goes hand in hand with the upcoming *Book Reviews that Matter.* I recognize we are gathering and processing so much information, and I so hope my overview is not overwhelming. My desire to bring a vital help in a simple form may fall short. Yet, validation is so integral to healthy minds and relationships; it connects our hearts. May this healing language renew your spirit of hope as you reach out to the heart of the hurting child you love so much.

References

Duckworth, Ken. "NAMI Honors Dr. Marsha Linehan, The Creator of Dialectical Behavior Therapy." *National Alliance on Mental Illness.* 5 October, 2015. Web. Originally published in NAMI's Fall 2015 *Advocate.* (www.nami.org)

Goleman, Daniel. *Emotional Intelligence.* New York: Bantam Books, 1995. Print.

Ginott, Dr. Haim. G. *Between Parent and Child: The Bestselling Classic that Revolutionized Parent-Child Communication.* Revised and Updated by Dr. Alice Ginott and Dr. H. Wallace Goddard. New York: Three Rivers Press, a member of the Crown Publishing Group, a division of Random House, Inc., 2003. Print.

Hall, Karyn D., Ph.D., and Melissa H. Cook, LPC. *The Power of Validation: Arming Your Child Against Bullying, Peer Pressure, Addiction, Self-Harm & Out-of-Control Emotions.* Oakland: New Harbinger Publications, Inc., 2012. Print.

Manning, Shari Y., Ph.D. *Loving Someone with Borderline Personality Disorder: How to Keep Out-of-control Emotions from Destroying Your Relationship.* New York: The Guilford Press, 2011. Print.

Porr, Valerie. *Overcoming Borderline Personality Disorder: A Family Guide for Healing and Change.* New York: Oxford University Press, Inc., 2010. Print.

CHAPTER SIX

Book Reviews that Matter

Taking a look at the most useful resources available to help us help our children will provide clarity and boost comprehension as we move forward. At first glance, this chapter might look like it belongs at the end of the book (I do share a slightly broader list of titles and websites in the Resources section). Each of the books featured here present direction and follow-up for building up our families, understanding our hurting children, and cultivating the language that is healing. I felt compelled to share these reviews sans delay. Going beyond symptoms of mental illness, medical terminology, and treatments of the disorders, these vital books additionally walk us through explanations and innumerable examples, taking us deeper into the principles of validation. The more we study, and the more illustrations we see, the better this concept will congeal, so we can modify our communication styles and foster improvement in well-being and relationships.

Prompting us toward empathy and effective communication, these authors take us by the hand and join us on the journey. They inspire compassion as they offer us heart and practical help in understanding and encouraging our loved ones. I cannot speak highly enough of the bounty of information and care they provide. As I mentioned, I've read countless books, yet am sharing what I believe to be the best when it comes to making *heart connections for true healing*.

Please keep an open mind and look beyond the titles. We are not prescribing medications here, simply ways to love and uplift our hurting children. So although your child may be struggling with depression, the message about validation in a book addressing borderline personality disorder may still provide help. In fact, I have found that although in psychological practice Dialectic Behavior Therapy is commonly used to help individuals with bipolar disorder, it is rarely mentioned in books specific to bipolar care. (This was our experience, and if you type that into your search engine, you'll find dozens of confirming resources.) Oddly, I have found more heart-rich books in the borderline field than in the bipolar. I hope there are still some promising options out there awaiting my discovery.

I heartily encourage you to read the books in full, yet in an effort to expedite healthier communications, I am unveiling just a few highlights. Most of these authors write with a passion and sensitivity born of their own painful experiences. The depth and wisdom is penetrating. It is my greatest hope that you will find help here. I continue to be grateful for the strength and support these vital lifelines have given me.

The Top Two

The first titles I'd like to introduce have resonated deeply within me with their messages of help and hope:

How I Stayed Alive When My Brain Was Trying to Kill Me: One Person's Guide to Suicide Prevention by Susan Rose Blauner. A powerful title introduces a profound book brimming with help, heart, and hope. The author speaks to the suicidal thinker, but we who love them can reap much benefit in the reading. She devotes a chapter to "Helping the Suicidal Thinker."

Because the danger of suicidal thinking is so prevalent in individuals with bipolar disorder, major depression, or borderline personality disorder, even if you do not believe this is pertinent to your situation now, reading a book like this could prove life-saving later. It is heartbreaking to read, but if you haven't entered into the abyss of the hurting heart of your child, her words may escort you there. As delicate as this is, we must be wise and brave, and not ignore this potentially devastating possibility.

I can't imagine a more thorough, more tender, all-encompassing resource on this most painful subject. I could just see my daughter all over this book, and wept through most of it. But it is beautiful and full of love.

Especially appreciate: In addition to statistics and a plethora of resources, Susan Rose Blauner teaches extensively on managing emotions. Blauner's writing delivers us into the deeps of the suicidal mind. When she writes of how she felt when suicidal, gripping and heart-wrenching descriptions touch us with pain for her, while delivering perspective on how our own children hurt.

This understanding, plus an awareness of signs and symptoms, can foster compassion and convict us of the necessity of opening up to conversations with our hurting children. She reminds us of the "extreme mental pain" of someone considering suicide (p. 243). Essentially, she explains how she "out-thought" her brain, and moved from suffering to hope; a hope so buoyant she now reaches out to encourage others and share affirmations for positive living. Blauner's song of life lies in the power of healing words. Her self-disclosure is illuminating: she helps us hear our children and promotes encouraging coping statements and healing words. In a section entitled: "What I Heard Versus What I Needed to Hear," she lists comments that did not help her, and offers more appropriate alternatives; she also shares a speech she gave which vividly demonstrates her point (pp. 233–236). Validation springs to life in her testimony. Blauner provides a broad range of helpful material that gets to the heart of healing and suicide prevention. As promised — heart, help, and hope overflow.

Everyone should probably read this book. I recommend you order a copy right away.

Overcoming Borderline Personality Disorder: A Family Guide for Healing and Change by Valerie Porr, M.A. Exceptional content, incredibly thorough, and genuinely instructive, this substantial work imparts compassion and beautifully teaches emotional language.

My heart connected with Valerie Porr's writing immediately. Her exhaustive work encompasses various elements of treatment that might be encountered, and she adeptly and thoroughly explains highly involved and multi-faceted concepts like dialectic behavior therapy, mindfulness, grief, radical acceptance, and so much more. The broad scope is amazing, yet explicitly detailed, and delivered with such tenderness.

Especially appreciate: Valerie Porr offers incredibly manageable, psychologically sound, seemingly simple counsel to us. For example, she highly recommends reflecting back for clarification and understanding: "Do I have this right?" or "Is this what you're saying?" (p. 147). She proposes we bolster healthier behavior by helping our kids remember previous successes as an encouragement to persevere and problem solve (p. 248). Poignant and compelling, Porr's teaching on validation encourages us to let our love flow and accept and understand whatever feelings our children may be experiencing. Although the specific subject of her fifth chapter, the concept and usage of validation is continually woven throughout her book.

Porr's interpretation of validation stirs my soul.

Next in Line

Loving Someone with Bipolar Disorder: Understanding and Helping Your Partner by Julie A. Fast and John D. Preston, Psy.D. Practical help, basic care, and good planning are outlined in this straightforward book. A holistic viewpoint grants us expanded vision and practicable action. Facts and particulars not commonly mentioned elsewhere are included. This book suggests creative ideas for healthy, proactive cooperation.

(Note: Fast and Preston write in reference to a spouse or partner, but I believe the reach extends beyond the title.)

Especially appreciate: Fast and Preston continually stress the basics, recommending examples of particular foods or types of exercise. They even underline the mental health benefits of keeping a tidy environment (pp. 58–60). Taking a holistic viewpoint, they give a nod to western medicine yet recognize alternative, nontraditional, measures that can help, such as acupuncture, herbs, chiropractic care, etc. They explain in a grounding manner the directive to respond instead of react when facing challenging issues (p. 56), expanding on this further in their eighth chapter, entitled "The Bipolar Conversation." A central premise Fast and Preston offer rests on action plans created *with* our loved ones when they are more stable to create a personal list of ideas for responses or beneficial activities to ease symptoms of mania, depression, paranoia, etc., when they recur.

The most noteworthy contribution this book made to my education, and the main reason it makes my top three, is the mind-body connection. In addition to their emphasis on the basics, the authors remark on the intense physical effect the disorder can have on the body, and also comment that our loved ones are more vulnerable to illness (pp. 57–58). I'm surprised at how many books on the subject fail to address these things. I wish I had known about these cues when my daughter had been a teen.

Their holistic approach to helping someone with such an illness is practical and caring.

Validation Essentials

To really learn, understand, and be better able to implement validation, I highly recommend *The Power of Validation* by Karyn Hall, Ph.D., and Melissa H. Cook, LPC. Although it is a parenting book, and not directed to families of children with mental illness, it provides exceptional direction. True, some of the stories might seem juvenile compared to the circumstances we currently face, but it facilitates comprehension, is concise, full of clear examples, thorough, and well-written. Take a look at the subtitle: *The Power of Validation: Arming Your Child Against Bullying, Peer Pressure, Addiction, Self-Harm & Out-of-Control Emotions.* Wow. That is *powerful*. A copy should be sent home in every kindergartner's backpack on the first day of school.

Dr. Hall has made a tremendous contribution to the validation conversation. A DBT clinician, Dr. Hall's prolific writings on mood management and more appear in various places online — in particular, a column for Psychology Today called *Pieces of Mind*, and one for PsychCentral entitled *The Emotionally Sensitive Person*. Additionally, she has published several books. For a quick overview, Karyn Hall has a feature in her *Pieces of Mind* column online at www.psychologytoday. com entitled "Understanding Validation: A Way to Communicate Acceptance." Internet articles might yield a good jump-start.

Clearly, I find Valerie Porr's *Overcoming Borderline Personality Disorder — A Family Guide for Healing and Change* to be an excellent study. While I ardently recommend Porr's book, I recognize this exhaustive work (it weighs in at around 350 pages) may feel like a "big read," especially if you're in crisis. You might just choose to read chapter five, and then select a few others.

Alternatively, I just recently discovered *Loving Someone with Borderline Personality Disorder: How to Keep Out-of-control Emotions from Destroying Your Relationship* by Shari Y. Manning, Ph.D., and found it to be very sound, sensitive, and direct. She teaches validation in chapter three of her book, and the ensuing chapter describes a step-by-step model for responding.

Validating Parenting

Again, to strengthen the principles of validation and bring it to life in our families, I feel these books can be beneficial no matter what the age of our children. If you are struggling with effective communication with a teen or adult child, they will be worthwhile; if you have younger children, these books are invaluable.

As discussed previously, *The Power of Validation: Arming Your Child Against Bullying, Peer Pressure, Addiction, Self-Harm & Out-of-Control Emotions,* by Karyn Hall, Ph.D., and Melissa H. Cook, LPC, is exemplary.

Although it doesn't specifically teach using the term "validation," support for validating parenting lies in *Between Parent and Child: The Best Selling Classic That Revolutionized Parent-Child Communication* by Dr. Haim Ginott, revised and updated (2003) by Dr. Alice Ginott and Dr. H. Wallace Goddard. I hunted and read untold books to find one that teaches such compassionate, relational parenting. His approach elegantly models validation. Even if you just read the intro and the first two chapters, I suspect you'll understand why I recommend this book no matter what age children are. (He has a teen version, but I much prefer this updated one.) I regularly suggest this book to parents of younger children, hoping that if mental illness or troubled teen years arise, they will be better equipped.

Vital for All of Us

The Depression Cure: The 6-Step Program to Beat Depression without Drugs by Dr. Stephen Ilardi, Ph.D. I believe this excellent book should be read by everyone. Not only essential for helping those who live with depression, the principles Dr. Ilardi prescribes are also key to managing stress. I have found his sage advice to be critical to coping with stress and fatigue. His chapter on the light box is worth the price of the book. (Please note, research indicates people with bipolar disorder risk increased chance of mania with lightbox usage. Consult with professional before use.) Although he writes with an intent to help people avoid medication, for those with more severe cases of mental illness, his ideas can supplement and provide benefit. With doctor's assent, many of Ilardi's prescriptives for healthy living that quell depression have been incorporated into our daughter's treatment program.

Also Reads

Helping Someone with Mental Illness: A Compassionate Guide for Family, Friends, and Caregivers by Rosalynn Carter with Susan K. Golant — a comprehensive book of mental illness. Although older (so some treatment, statistics, and legal information is not up-to-date), this straightforward and sensitive book remains a superb first encounter with the broad range of issues related to mental illness. It covers basic definitions, prevalence, national perspectives, stigma, various disorders, encouragement for caregivers, questions about prevention, advocacy, and more.

Emotional Intelligence by Daniel Goleman — in a class by itself — this book is not about mental illness, yet Goleman's insight and research on emotions and developing skills to manage them are right in line with the efforts we are making as we encourage our hurting children. I agree wholeheartedly with his call to "emotional education." His report encompasses emotional wellness from the home, into the the school, the workplace, and beyond. Probably one of my favorite books in any genre; really important contribution to understanding humanity.

From My Daughter's Bookshelf

I Hate You Don't Leave Me: Understanding the Borderline Personality, by Jerold. J. Kreisman, MD, and Hal Straus. This book does a superior job of defining borderline personality disorder and the unhealthy behaviors that can accompany it. My daughter and I both really appreciated the second chapter, "Chaos and Emptiness," for its account of the intense pain and confusion experienced by individuals with this diagnosis.

Memoir Reservoir: I've read numerous memoirs; they are challenging for me. Witnessing my daughter's struggles has been excruciatingly painful. Reading someone else's pain hurts me twice: as I hurt for the heart of the writer, and as I recognize the similarities with my daughter. They tend to fill me with sadness. We are all different, so you might wish to pursue this genre to better understand your child. But I'd like to share that these books speak to my daughter's heart, helping her feel a comradeship, and a sense she's not alone. My. That seems … validating.

Book End

The common thread of these books is the *heart* involved. Supporting us as we open up with deep, energizing, compassionate connection — these books deliver. Without being too clinical, they explain the medical and psychological background; they share practical measures; and they express a deep sense of caring. They each stress the importance of listening. In addition, each book offers a chapter about taking care of ourselves which is very kind and supportive (a subject matter omitted by many). These authors are devoted to helping us understand, communicate, and connect. And that connection channels life and love and healing into our children's souls.

These books and additional resources are listed in Resources.

CHAPTER SEVEN

Coaching Life

I believe as parents, we are our children's life coaches. And for our children with emotional disorders, we are not only called to life coaching, we are called to be *coaching life*.

We teach, we learn with them, we encourage, we guide, we try and try again, we come alongside them, and sometimes we just hold their hands. We plant seeds of hope that we can cultivate in the hearts and minds of our children as they grow and develop. We want our children to bloom as mature, independent people with self-sustaining skills, equipped to become beautiful individuals living full lives of purpose and joy. Maybe we feel very far away from that goal right now, but keeping the goals in sight might motivate us in the dark days to persevere in caring and coaching and hoping. If we desire to reach the hearts of our children with touches that foster health and safety and hope, we coach life to them through many avenues. These include: emotional, physical, mental, and spiritual.

Coaching Life – Emotionally

The core of this small book brings emotional support to light …

We pour out love and compassion. From the wellsprings of love, we lean in closely with one of the greatest gifts a soul can give: listening. True, active, engaged, listening from the heart. We encourage the discussion of feelings and validate the emotions. We tend to their hearts.

Coaching Life – Physically

As parents, most of us are generally quite accustomed to providing for the physical needs of our children. The list of what we do is endless, and the care we give our hurting children may require a different component or two. Initially, we start with the basics of good health Furthermore, we coach our kids in the physical respect by promoting healthful, pleasant pursuits. And finally, we can assist and support in navigating the medication and counseling territories.

Essential Care

Basic care is so essential, the message bears repeating. We've found at least six components critical to healing and nourishing better mental health:

- the basics:
  - nutrition
  - sleep
  - exercise
- medication
- good counseling
- something productive to do
- a safe place to live
- the presence of loving, caring, supportive people

Our daughter needs to be in balance in *every area* in order to move forward sometimes. The slightest change — like daylight savings time — can present challenges. It is a very delicate dance.

Physical pain can accompany emotional pain. This has been true in our case, and something I wish I had known earlier in the journey. My daughter often quotes her counselor: "Mind affects body; body, mind." Extra doctors' appointments may be required to pursue concerns and ascertain causes.

Distractivities

Yep, that's right: distracting + activities = distractivities.

Sometimes small, simple actions are the only way to tiptoe forward. Until we were attempting to survive the depths of grief while struggling with the height of fear, we had never understood that "fake it 'til you make it" *is a plan*. And the only way through — through what for us has been YEARS — has been through the tiniest little increments imaginable.

While distraction gets a bad reputation for resembling its evil twin cousin denial, we certainly found distractivities to be a way forward while trying to cope, waiting to breathe, and striving for hope. Sometimes "play" provides a welcome distraction. We can create meaningful times of togetherness, explore new hobbies, enjoy family events, and plan and engage in fun activities. We might: prepare a meal together, volunteer to do something nice for somebody else, or get pedicures (pricey, but oh, so lovely); we might have family movie or game night, or visit a favorite painting at the art gallery, and sit in front of it for thirty full minutes. Family game night isn't going to erase their pain or heal their wounds, yet it's a small way to build up life-giving promise, and remind ourselves that in the midst of hard times, sometimes it's appropriate to make an effort to invite pleasurable times.

You probably already know that sometimes your child might not want to participate. Sometimes the depression prevents it. Sometimes it is okay for them to have time alone. None of these things are wild prescriptions, and in the throes of crisis all bets are off, but in the long, quiet, aching stretches, these types of activities have helped us inch along.

Advanced Care

When it comes to medication and counseling, depending upon the age and capabilities of our children, we can help with rudimentary elements, such as picking up prescriptions, driving to appointments, and gently reminding our loved ones to take the medicine. The following notes from our family's website, www. thebraveheartconnection.com, share further insight.

- Accept the treatment program. For many parents, accepting the diagnosis is difficult. It can also be challenging to accept the fact that your son or daughter requires medication and therapy. Perhaps quite a few different medicines. I understand. But we are trying to save our children, and these medications may be integral to their well-being. Lay your fears to rest. There is no shame in it; please know it is okay, and reassure your child that it is okay to need and take these medicines. Glasses are prescribed for vision correction; a person with diabetes needs insulin. Similarly, medications may be necessary for our children as they climb toward balance and health. A medication regime can greatly enhance the success of therapy. Accept, and be a part of the healing team.

- It is wise to have an overview of medicines frequently prescribed. Please refer to a psychiatrist, reputable books, or trustworthy websites for information on particular medications, usage, and side effects.

- If the medication regimen is new to your family, anticipate ongoing psychiatric care. Although there are still psychiatrists who provide counseling, from what we're seeing, it is most common to have a counselor for therapy sessions, in addition to a psychiatrist for medication needs. So, yes, we not only need to search for a counselor, we need to search for a psychiatrist or a physician to prescribe.

- Essentially, this means we are building a team of caring individuals. We have shared contact information between our psychologist and psychiatrist, and they have conferred with one another on several occasions, which has been very helpful.

- Be prepared for medication issues. Medications can take a while to begin to work. Side effects thwart the use of many. In other cases, a certain medicine doesn't seem to do the job, so the psychiatrist will change the prescription. In our experience, changing one often means changing another. Finding the right balance can take time, and even so, changes may be required after a while. At times, our children may want to quit taking the medicines … sometimes because of side effects; sometimes due to irritation with the challenges; and sometimes because they are feeling better, so they feel they don't need them! Continual monitoring is entailed. It can be frustrating, but hold on to hope!

- Cultivate a relationship with the pharmacist. Pharmacists are so highly trained, and are generally accessible by phone. We have called with specific questions about medications and side effects, yet also about personal situations such as adding over-the-counter cold medicines, or what do if there has been a medication mess up (missed pill, wrong pill, etc). Our pharmacists have always been very friendly and willing to help us, beyond what we might have expected; they have spent quite a bit of time on the phone answering questions, and been very compassionate. We have also received some ideas about working with our insurance company, and one even attempted to help us obtain some coupons (unsuccessful, but very kind).

- Consider requesting a partial prescription filling. Our daughter is very sensitive to medications, and has experienced awful side effects with many. Because we have been working with a number of different medications in an effort to find the most beneficial combination, we early realized that the medicines that were not right for her were then a non-returnable waste of money. So upon receiving a new prescription, we sometimes request a *partial* filling at the pharmacy, like a week's worth. Frequently, unpleasant side effects have shown up immediately, so this plan has saved us considerably. ***Important note:*** Always contact the psychiatrist about any side effects right away to discuss what steps to take. Occasionally, ours has encouraged us to give it more time; usually, we see him again and he prescribes an alternative.

Again, finding the balance can be painstaking, but it is so necessary in helping our children to better health.

- Practice safe medicine storage. If you have younger children, it is advisable to have a locked medicine cabinet. This also may be wise if you are worried about your child misusing the medicine. Because our daughter used her own prescriptions in her nearly fatal suicide attempt, she currently only keeps a week's worth of pills on hand. That gives us peace of mind. Better yet, it was her idea.

Notes about Counseling

The importance of having a good counselor cannot be overstated. A good counselor is a lifeline.

However, it's a very delicate situation. Not only do we hope for a good therapist, but there needs to be some degree of connection. We've learned a patient needs to like or feel comfortable with a counselor. Quite a combination of personalities, relationships, skills, and effort comes together to foster health and healing.

It requires so much strength, courage, and energy to enter into counseling. Upon entering, we carry such hope — it can be crushing when it is not a good match. And unfortunately, it is exhausting to make a counseling change. It can be incredibly intense for our children — and for us, when we are walking through this with them — beginning again, reliving and sharing the past, bringing a new counselor into the present situation, asking questions, trying to get to know each other …

Over the years, we wasted much time and money on counseling for our daughter that didn't help. Unbeknownst to us, we spent much time with a poor counselor. We've had counseling "disconnects," counseling misdiagnosis, a counselor who moved away at a critical time, a counselor in over his head, and even a counselor who fired us!

No wonder people can be reluctant. No wonder, in spite of terrible pain, that people choose not to go. Understanding this can build our sense of compassion, yet our caring hearts comprehend we must continue to seek help for our children. We must press on.

When our daughter agreed to get back into counseling (as a young adult) her grief and illness depleted her of energy or motivation to seek help, so I took on the search for a therapist. Numerous phone calls and telephone interviews ensued — most counselors were very gracious about phoning me back and answering questions. My own education on mental illness, treatment, and specific therapies proved helpful in identifying our needs and formulating questions. We had other concerns to weigh, as well, and created a checklist chart to facilitate the process (this chart can be downloaded from our website). After briefly explaining our daughter's struggle and most recent diagnosis, we asked about specific types of therapies utilized, if the therapist had evening hours, and phone accessibility. And, of course, we asked the insurance and payment questions. (Some counselors offer sliding scale fees.) Additionally, we considered geography, because frequent sessions that involve leaving work or children, etc., coupled with a lengthy drive could eventually prove a hindrance to keeping appointments.

Two other notes regarding counseling:

- If we are uncertain about any diagnosis or treatment plan, we must trust those instincts and be tenacious. We know our own children. It can be tiring, but we might need to consult with more than one care provider, or ask more questions.

- If our children are minors, they will be meeting with the counselor privately. In our experience, the parents are generally included at the beginning or the end of the session for updates or discussion of issues. Once our children are over 18, it is up to them to include us, and to sign paperwork that permits the counselor to speak directly with us. Bear in mind, most counseling offices have a provision for a "family appointment," which will not jeopardize counselor/patient confidentiality, but opens up an opportunity for family members to learn what can be done at home to support and encourage their loved one.

Coaching Life – Mentally

As parents, we hope that all of our children will garner the skills to cope well with the challenges and pains of life. Our loved ones with bipolar disorder, major depression, or borderline personality disorder need every extra measure possible to calm emotions and facilitate healthy brain activity, shifting processing from the emotional area (amygdala) to the rational, thinking part (prefrontal cortex).

If our words and responses can help our loved ones break a chain of negative thought processes, let's do what we can. Although we so dearly desire to prevent self-harming thoughts and behaviors, we nevertheless must recognize we can't be responsible for their thoughts. Or their actions. But I, for one, want to know I have done everything I possibly could to help. At the end of the day, no matter the circumstances, I need to be at peace with myself.

So we continually strive to nourish and mentally feed our hurting children. Personally, I'm interested in any measures that can be taken to sow more positive growth and healing. Next, in a very condensed fashion, we'll look over some simple but powerful ideas.

The Question Suggestion and Its Intention

Through trial and error I discovered as my kids became teenagers that it was generally more helpful to phrase comments as questions rather than state my opinion or tell them what to do. Effectual and practical, the art of asking questions turns out to be an important parenting tool. Learning about validation and various therapies has solidified in my mind the significance of this special ability.

Who knew?

Questions help us think. This is nothing new — Socrates employed this process with his students over two thousand years ago. The Socratic method is still used to teach critical thinking skills. Naturally, we are not attempting to enter into debate or intense discourse — we are merely hoping to realign thought processes and encourage logical thinking over emotional thinking. And compassionate questions can help.

Initially, our questions may simply be seeking the emotional status of our child: "How are you feeling about that?" "Can you describe what you are feeling?" "Tell me why you're angry …"

And after lovingly listening to and validating our hurting children, we begin to ask questions. Gentle and engaged, we ask get-to-the-heart questions that can (hopefully) lead to understanding, perspective, and wise resolutions. (These types of guiding questions are recommended in the books by Fast and Preston, Blauner, Porr, and more.) The questions should arise naturally and be heartfelt, with care and love at the core.

- Do you want to talk more about it?

- How can I help?

- What do you really need right now?

- What are you planning to do?

- What are your options?

Patiently, we try to help them help themselves. As they struggle with some issue or incident, can we help them reframe a situation, and find another perspective? Can we ask them to evaluate their actions and consider alternatives? Or perhaps we can ask questions that help them to recognize they did the best they could, therefore shifting the focus toward a strength. At a certain appropriate point in conversation, or if they get stuck, we might ask if they'd like to hear another idea (see Porr, 2010, p. 134). Then we can share, and ask what they think.

Resulting conversations like this fall under the umbrella of healthy communication. The questions work to steer them toward discernment and independence. Ultimately, we want our children to be able to make healthy choices on their own accord.

Refresh the Mindset

The expression "positive thinking" may sound overly cheerful, trite, or light for our purposes — especially when we are in the darkest of circumstances, so sensitive timing is helpful. Yet we are hoping to validate, love, and *refresh a mindset* with positive thoughts that may yield more positive energy or confidence, ideally nurturing promise and success in coping and making sound choices. The fact is, we *all* need more positive and hopeful thoughts reverberating in our heads. Again, this is not a remedy. Simply another tiny step toward healthy living.

We have created mantras that are powerful and motivating to us, and that we use regularly to hearten ourselves. Small as it may seem, these messages carry some weight as we attempt to encourage our girl through dark or challenging times. One of them is: "Hurts like hell, but we are strong." We often remind ourselves: "We've been through worse." I also adopted a line from Valerie Porr, and point out to my daughter that she "can do hard things" (Porr, 2010, p. 337). My dear one recently began reciting to herself that "Feelings, no matter how strong, are temporary." These thoughts have carried us through many a rough time.

Positive thinking and affirmations can engender healing help. Susan Rose Blauner takes much encouragement through them, and collects sayings from famous people, song lyrics, the Twelve Steps program, even fortune cookies. She shares a list of these affirmations, plus some of her own, in her book (Blauner, 2002, pp. 167–169). She uses these messages to encourage herself and finds they truly help "reassure the brain" (p. 166).

Keeping conversations open, and pouring out love, we might coach our loved ones with uplifting and promising messages that can promote stamina and hope. Countless websites offer encouragement and positive messages. Many books share daily positive meditations or affirmations. I always seek books, yet strengthening thoughts have come to me from unexpected places like a random radio message, a billboard, a children's book, and even book titles — (I've recently been pondering "courage grows strong at the wound" from the title of a book by Robert C. Koehler that I haven't even read yet!) Extending beyond affirmations, we might share novels, poems, songs, or even theater performances. My daughter has found tremendous strength and inspiration from Kahlil Gibran's exquisite poem, "On Joy and Sorrow." We may collect inspiring thoughts and quotes, and gather them into a notebook, create posters for the walls, or write them on sticky notes and place them all around. As I uncover gems that I feel might especially touch my daughter I write them down on 4 × 6 notecards for her. At Christmas, I select the most powerful and eloquent quotations, and print and frame them for each of my children.

Another manner in which we can help our children find healing brain space is through encouraging them to journal. Writing down feelings and thoughts has proven to be a very therapeutic outlet of expression, and journaling is recommended by almost every expert. Maybe we gently suggest; maybe we furnish lovely new notebooks or pens.

My daughter's counselor taught her a very interesting technique I refer to as the and/but/yet sentence. We take a truthful statement that may express some emotion or problem, and we counter it by adding an "and/but/yet" truth. For example:

- I feel really sad, but I'm still going to dinner with my friends.

- This scares me, and I'm doing it, anyway.

- My depression has really kicked in, but I know there are things I can do to cope.

- I don't feel well, and I'm still going to work.

- I don't like this, yet I'm strong enough to make it through.

Essentially, we state two truths that are linked together by one of these conjunctions. The two clauses of the sentence may appear to conflict, contrast, or even be opposites, but they are both true. The first part of the sentence usually relates to emotions or distressing circumstances, and the second part counters it with some positive message, strengthening action, or hopeful truth. These and/but/yet clauses (*and* is the nucleus) can be affirming, assertive, and even uplifting. We can help our children learn to cope, coach, and encourage themselves by working with them to create fortifying sentences or mantras that can build their confidence, and lead them to stronger places. It is so subtle; so simple — yet so strengthening! *It is empowering.*

Embrace the Dialectical

Further reading indicates this "and/but/yet" technique exemplifies Marsha Linehan's Dialectical Behavior Therapy (DBT). The word dialectical is defined by www.merriam-webster.com as "the dialectical tension or opposition between two interacting forces or elements." Google.com posts: "concerned with or acting through opposing forces."

This sheds significant light on the and/but/yet sentence skill. It's such a manageable exercise, and the counterbalance seems potent.

Originally developed by Dr. Linehan to help suicidal individuals and people with borderline personality disorder, Dialectical Behavior Therapy (DBT) is now used to treat other mood disorders and conditions, as well. (This may explain why so many of the books that address it have "borderline" in the title.) It is a multi-faceted, full, and impressive therapy, with a variety of components. Because it can be so vital to helping our kids, I recommend at least a small attempt at learning about DBT. Although a summary of the therapy is not feasible here, very comprehensible explanations can be found through the experts. (Valerie Porr's work is detailed and explicit; or refer to Shari Manning, or others mentioned in Resources.) A slightly different approach is a very useful handbook: *The Dialectic Behavior Therapy Skills Workbook: Practical DBT Exercises for Learning Mindfulness, Interpersonal Effectiveness, Emotion Regulation & Distress Tolerance* by Matthew McKay, Ph.D., Jeffrey C. Wood, Psy.D., Jeffrey Brantley, MD.

Intended for the person struggling with what they refer to as "overwhelming emotions," this handbook is a very easy-to-use tool for those of us who are loving someone with such disorders. As a workbook, it does not put forth the full psychological exposition of the therapy; rather, it presents lessons and exercises to directly and efficaciously teach fundamental skills. Not only can this book help us understand what our children might be learning in therapy, but the exercises give excellent guidance to us in coaching our kids. The authors inculcate strategies for coping during times of stress or crisis, and emphasize the need to break existing patterns of thought or habits. They submit examples of what they call "coping thoughts," (which reflect the concept of affirmations and and/but/yet sentences) and they suggest choosing or creating key coping thoughts to rely on and recite (pp. 11, 47–49, 150). Much more is covered, as they supply further questions, advice, and exercises. We might seek feedback from our child's counselor about using this workbook, as well. It can greatly enhance our understanding and efforts to help.

Just to provide an iota of familiarity, a few terms we encounter when studying DBT include: distress tolerance skills, radical acceptance, and mindfulness. DBT is a very specialized therapy, and I should mention that not all practitioners have the proper training. It is an important question to ask when searching for a good counselor. (A number of other therapies are described in the books, as well. In addition to DBT, Cognitive Behavior Therapy and Acceptance and Commitment Therapy are two of those with which we have had some experience in counseling.)

We can't be our children's therapists, and we may not have the time or the inclination to gain expertise in the subject, but even some rudimentary knowledge will bolster our capacity to help. Our hearts may be full of pain and hope simultaneously, but with love and persistence, perhaps some of our coaching will eventually be adopted and adapted by our children, so that they will in time self-coach, self-encourage, and cope better.

A review of this section may revitalize us: We gently and lovingly guide with questions; we want to refresh the mindset with positive, strengthening affirmations or mantras; we can empower our children with coping statements, using and/but/yet as a pattern; and we can take cues from Dialectical Behavior Therapy.

We engage, we connect, we empower.

Coaching Life – Spiritually

The professionals don't often mention the role of faith in the books, but as we are trying to foster good health in every way, we may also want to recognize the spirituality of our children. Prayer and meditation can lead to hope and wisdom, and islands of peace — if only for a moment. Kindly remember, our children may not believe what we believe. Depending upon the circumstances they've encountered, and the depths of their pain, this can be a dark time in faith. In hard times, we are all challenged and stretched uncomfortably.

We need to encourage them with what speaks to their depths.

If we share the same beliefs, this will be easier. With our children's assent, we might pray together, derive inspiration from spiritual texts, and enlist support from people within our faith community. If our children believe differently, keep in mind, there is pain, possibly crisis involved, and this not the time for theological debate or pleading. Remember our theme: we are speaking to their hearts; speaking the language that lifts and heals. We might need to be creative, but we can search for some respectful way to express, connect, or participate together.

I briefly mentioned journaling earlier. In our family, we've been counseled routinely to keep gratitude journals. Calling to mind and writing down things for which we're thankful builds hope. It can help us focus, grant perspective, and, during darker days, serve as a reminder of better moments. Some people might take off with this; if our loved one doesn't, we might be able to collaborate. We can work together to identify what is good in life, acknowledging the bright spots — maybe a new medicine is helping, or we enjoyed time together at a family celebration. Cultivating gratitude in their hearts may be the simplest whisper of delight in something beautiful. Continue to seek even the tiniest treasures with them, and in time this may seep into their souls.

We can strengthen their hearts by feeding them tender, loving, positive messages that encourage perseverance, hope, and courage.

References

Blauner, Susan Rose. *How I Stayed Alive When My Brain Was Trying to Kill Me: One Person's Guide to Suicide Prevention.* New York: Quill, an imprint of HarperCollins Publishers, 2002. Print.

McKay, Matthew, Ph.D., Jeffrey C. Wood, Psy.D., and Jeffrey Brantley, MD. *The Dialectic Behavior Therapy Skills Workbook: Practical DBT Exercises for Learning Mindfulness, Interpersonal Effectiveness, Emotion Regulation & Distress Tolerance.* Oakland: New Harbinger Publishers, Inc., 2007. Print.

Porr, Valerie. *Overcoming Borderline Personality Disorder: A Family Guide for Healing and Change.* New York: Oxford University Press, Inc., 2010. Print.

www.thebraveheartconnection.com.

CHAPTER EIGHT

The 4-1-1 on the 9-1-1

My daughter responds:

What am I like when I am depressed and suicidal?

My body is a cage that my mind is trapped inside. This is how I feel when my darkness has arrived.

I am blind. When I am depressed and suicidal, I am blind. The beauty of nature? I do not see. The love in my mother's eyes? I do not see. My friends' concerned faces? I do not see. I see nothing but darkness. I hardly believe anything but that exists. I am lost, fumbling around, searching for something, anything, to hold onto. But there is nothing. There is desperation, guilt, confusion, self-hatred and pain, always pain. And often times, in my blindness, I lose hope of ever being able to see again. I forget what having sight is like. There is no light. There is no way out. And in these moments I want nothing more than to end my pathetic excuse for a life.

I am deaf. When I am depressed and suicidal, I am deaf. The gentle sounds of the city waking up in the morning? I do not hear. The music that captivates me? I do not hear. The loving words spoken to me? I do not hear. Instead I am alone with the whispers of my mind, doubts and fear, a ringing in my ears. I drown in poisonous lies; the pain I feel is my own fault. I am a pathetic pile of shit. I am untouchable, forgettable, unfixable, regrettable. All I hear is my own demons, turning on themselves. There is no hope in the words of my thoughts. Only hatred, only sorrow, only pain. The only answer I can be given, the only one that is shrieking inside my head, the only thing I come *close* to hearing is this: *end it. Your life is worth nothing.*

I am mute. When I am depressed and suicidal, I am mute. The truth? I cannot speak it. Help? I cannot ask for it. My sadness? I cannot explain it. I feel like I am screaming and no sound is coming out. Like I am alone inside a bubble and those around me hear nothing. I give up trying. I am not worth being heard. In my darkest hour, I hold only sick beliefs. So I am alone, crying with silence, curling up in a ball, holding my head in my hands. I wish I were dead.

I am numb. When I am depressed and suicidal, I am numb. The first cool breeze of Autumn against my cheeks? I do not feel it. The warmth of a loved ones embrace? I do not feel it. The pleasure of being a lover? I do not feel it. All I want is to be held, kissed on the forehead, or rocked back and forth. I can run for miles, I can slit my wrists open, I can whip myself with a belt until I chip one of my ribs. But there is only nothingness. There is no hand to hold. There is no release for the pain that is mercilessly ripping me apart inside. There is nowhere for it to go, so it spins itself around inside of me, breaking and tearing me inside my wounded skin. Death would not be painful; I wouldn't feel a thing. And so begins the fantasizing.

When I am depressed and suicidal, I am blind, I am deaf, I am mute, I am numb.

My body is a cage that my mind is trapped inside. But on the outside, I smile and answer, "I'm fine".

Oh, the ache of this mother's heart.

Tragically, for many of us, loving and living with someone with bipolar disorder, major depression, or borderline personality disorder at some point entails physical injury and suicide threats or attempts.

Perhaps if parents can access good books and support and implement vital communication skills early on, they can be spared the worst. I don't know. But I hope so.

For those of us caught up in living the crisis-driven life, and for those who want to be wise and be prepared, the following information might be helpful. When our children become distressed and experience intense pain, often their sensitive souls perceive a crisis, and their response to that anguish is harmful, dangerous, or life-threatening. We must do all that we can to help them be safe. First, we must always, ALWAYS take a suicide threat seriously.

First, we must always, ALWAYS
take a suicide threat seriously.

That is the most important thing to remember. From here, one might contact the counselor, call a suicide prevention hotline, call 911, or go to the emergency room. *We must learn much more about suicide prevention in order to be better prepared for this terrible situation.*

If our loved ones are struggling with suicidal thoughts, we need to be knowledgeable and proactive. We want every resource on board to help us help our children in this most dire situation. The websites and hotlines listed in Resources relay credible and valuable assistance. I recommend becoming familiar with the material given on a variety of suicide prevention websites. These not only post dangerous signs and statistics, but also guidelines for conversations and questions for us to ask. Many people are hindered by the myth that bringing suicide up may cause a hurting person to think about it, but avoiding the subject does not help our loved ones. We are, in fact, instructed to ask very targeted questions like "Are you thinking about suicide?" and "Do you have a plan?" I first learned this through a counselor, and it was hard! My baby seemed so young! There is no "too young" in this regard. So we must be brave. It is crucial. Our children's lives are at risk. The websites propose many more questions, and they differ slightly in ideas, information, and presentation. That is why I recommend reviewing several of them. Fill your brain, so you can be ready on the spot … awful as it is.

The hotline phone numbers can be very helpful. We wish we had known that *these lines are not just for the individuals considering suicide.* We who love and support them can also call for help and consultation.

(I called them to make sure; they were very gracious.) When we call, there's a brief recording and just the slightest wait before we are on the line with a real person. They attempt to connect us with a local contact. You may also obtain a number for your local county agency, as well. They offer assistance, and may have knowledge of institutions, resources, and support groups nearby.

I recommend memorizing these numbers: 1.800.273.TALK and 1.800.SUICIDE.

Please remember the work of Susan Rose Blauner. In her book, she shares many of the suggestions from the suicide prevention organizations. Her work fosters compassion and can renew our efforts in addressing such deep pain and speaking love that heals. As I've said, I cannot imagine a more thorough, more tender, all-encompassing book that could prove to be life-saving. It is amazing.

Nothing can describe the agony of a child's suicidality. Please, *please* explore the resources given to equip yourself as much as possible. Also, because we received no support or information whatsoever from the hospitals after our daughter's suicide attempts, I was prompted to write: *How to Cope When Your Loved One is in the Psychiatric Hospital*, available at amazon.com.

Leaving someone we love in the psychiatric hospital is incredibly hard. So much pain is involved; and we had no idea what to expect. I share insight gleaned during our hospital experiences, in addition to practical help and caring companionship similar to what you've read here. If your son or daughter is struggling with suicidal thoughts, you might consider this booklet, as well as the book by Susan Rose Blauner.

The extreme pain of our hurting children requires extreme parenting. Many of us live and practice suicide prevention every day. My daughter would be the first to tell you that her momma has saved her life. More than once. And that leads me to the hardest thing I have to say. The path toward healing is not a straight line. The ups and downs of the journey through the shadows continually grip us. The heart-palpitating truth we have lived compels me to write, to share with you as another one in the fray, holding onto hope, yet ricocheting into panic alternatively. You already know the most dreadful possibility. We are not in control. We don't know what is going to happen … We can't predict the unpredictability of these illnesses … We cannot anticipate the dangers or the depths … And we don't know when overpowering darkness might set in and our beautiful child may despairingly choose to leave us. We cannot always save them. Too many grieving families testify to this. The high numbers of lives so tragically lost is numbing. Yet I, personally, am driven to do everything I can, knowing that no matter what happens, I have to be able to live with myself.

Our daughter's teen years were fraught with pain and moods and identity crises. She struggled with self-harming behaviors and had threatened suicide many times. In college, the roller coaster ride of emotions, relationship issues, and self-destructive thoughts and behaviors continued. Then life hit us with a shattering blow beyond imagination.

So much of the heartache we have experienced with our daughter has occurred while we've been grieving the loss of a baby to SIDS. This daughter's baby; our first grandchild. The devastation of losing a child, to us, seems unparalleled. Enduring such tragedy, coupled with the terror of losing our daughter to suicide, seemed impossible. It has been a nightmare. We have lived in constant fear and anguish.

We barely breathed through so many years of confusion, pain, and sorrow; and our daughter lived in a place of unspeakable darkness and emotional torment. Every day was excruciating for her. Her mind was frantic to escape life. She attempted suicide three times, and nearly died the third time. From there it has been a long and tumultuous course before she ultimately made the decision to choose life.

How long will this occupy such a prominent place in our psyches?

We don't know. We valiantly struggle onward, grateful that now our girl has appropriate medications, a good counselor, and a new outlook. We are hopeful. Yet we are still learning the many faces of mental illness, and the fear of suicide has been deeply ingrained.

In the event that it might be helpful to you, I want to share a personal prayer from my mother's heart in the depths of distress. Reciting some variation of this is how I ended every day for years … night after night after night after long and tearful night. It was the only way I could close my eyes and hope for sleep.

Dear Heavenly Father – I am scared and worried about my girl. I pray, dear God, that she will not take her own life tonight. Dear God, I love her. You know how much this hurts. I pray for her safety and well-being. I am tired and I am hurting, and I need to go to bed. Dear Lord, I put her in your hands. Take care of her; she's Your child, too. Please take care of us all. Bless my family. Grant me peace that comes with believing I have done everything I could do today. Amen.

CHAPTER NINE

Coping

Up to this point we have been focusing on helping and encouraging our hurting children. It is a road strewn with pain. While the challenges may seem daunting, I hope this small book has helped you to see the scope of the mission before us, and to begin to access ideas and resources that will equip us in making a positive difference. On top of this, however, we also need to learn ways to cope as we traverse this rocky terrain.

So for a moment, we are going to look toward our own inner landscape and consider how to tend to our needs and build a healthy, supportive foundation for hope and endurance. In this chapter I share what I have done, and how I continue to try to cope. I simply offer these suggestions to you.

I believe these keys hold the significant and sustaining measures for coping:

- Rest

- Wrestle

- Resilience

Rest

We are all affected by the pain our loved one feels. Perhaps life has been very trying and stressful for quite some time. Even as we provide care for our children, we must allow ourselves to pay attention to our needs, as well. So as we coach our children to start with the basics of all good health — proper nutrition, exercise, and sleep — we must acknowledge that these factors are also crucial to *our* well-being and strength. We tend to our darlings; we must tend to ourselves, too. It is so easy to let these things- even the most essential human needs — drop by the wayside. But we must maintain optimum health in order to have strength for the journey. I emphasize this because I have failed miserably here! It is so hard!

Be warned: the stresses can take a toll. Two of us were diagnosed with Adrenal Fatigue Syndrome. It took a long time to recover from that. If we had been more mindful of the most elementary care, perhaps it could have been avoided. Or it might not have been as severe. If you have long been living in crisis, grief, or distress, you may also be a victim. I recommend you investigate this and speak with your doctor about taking action for better health.

It is very important to give ourselves permission to slow things down, really rest, and take care of our needs in order to be strengthened for the future. How we create these opportunities will vary. I heard people saying, "Take care of yourself!" and all I could think was, "How do I do that??" For a long time, I couldn't even fathom what that meant! My concerns for my daughter's well-being, and my desire to take care of all of my children to the best of my ability seemed so large in my mind.

Worry and stress can make rest and self-care seem impossible. Unfortunately, there is no panacea. I discovered it happens through very tiny steps. Through the years, my daughter and I have learned many small but helpful ways to combat anxiety and stress. Some very beneficial techniques:

- *Deep breathing* – (I found myself doing this before I knew it was a technique!) Breathe in slowly through the nose, hold for an equal count, then release through pursed lips to a longer, slower count. It physiologically slows down brain activity, decreases heart rate, and may possibly lower blood pressure. Repeat often.

- *Counting* – Yes, count things. This may sound nuts, but when your mind is far away, worrying about your loved one's mental health and dangerous behavior, you can stay immersed in the present by counting things. Count whatever is in your vicinity: stop lights, red cars, green books, flowers in the wallpaper, etc.

- *Tossing the ball* – An excellent counselor explained to us the underlying principle behind treatment for post-traumatic stress involves engaging each half of the brain alternately, which helps facilitate brain processing. (For more information, research EMDR therapy.) I just borrowed this one portion of EMDR, and noticed some relief. Find a small, yet weighty ball (a yoga ball or stress-ball at discount stores is about $5), and toss it from one hand to the other. As the ball crosses the centerline of the body, touching one hand and then the other, it effects change in the brain.

- *Play Doh* – Another therapist taught us this one for decreasing frustration and stress: pound it, mold it, smash it, stab it with a plastic knife …

- *Water* – Water can be soothing, and refreshing. Take a break to wash your face. Close your eyes and let your skin get drenched in a shower or bubble bath. Dip into a pool or splash your feet in a lake. Slow down and sit near a local pond or other body of water.

- *Nature* – Get outside, take in a view, watch a butterfly, listen to the leaves rustle in the wind, breathe in fresh air, hike, bask in the warmth of the sun. I personally find great peace and restoration in nature.

- *Art* – Grab the crayons, paint, or pencils, and dive in. Expressing herself through all kinds of artistic (and musical) outlets has afforded my daughter immense comfort and healing.

- *Lavender* – This scent has calming properties. Try it in candles, lotions, scented pillows.

Additionally, experiment with other elements that promote relaxation such as herbal teas, scented candles, gentle exercise, swinging on a swing, rocking in a rocking chair, soothing music, massage, etc.

Wrestle

Our loved one hurts, and we hurt, too. Some of us have encountered terrible and unbelievably tough circumstances, beyond what we ever could have imagined when we entered parenthood. We may be entrenched in the world of mental illness, witnessing much pain and darkness, and preparing for a lifetime of concern. We want to be hopeful, but we're scared. We don't know what might happen next.

Over the years, I have spoken with several experts, read copious website articles, and pored over countless books to glean any helpful coping skills. Please remember my disclaimer: I am not a doctor and the following ideas are not a substitute for professional help. While many represent my own personal responses, most of the concepts highlighted are found in a large number of publications on mental illness, self-help, grief and recovery. I have assimilated and appreciated it all.

Whatever your circumstances, I hope these thoughts lead to help and hope.

Wrestle with your own emotions:

Faced with the task of tending to a seriously distressed loved one and nurturing positive living intentions, we still have our own feelings to manage. At times we may find ourselves feeling completely overwhelmed. Take heed. Look carefully at yourself and your particular circumstances. I advise you to seek professional counsel for dealing with the stress of chronic crisis management.

On top of our children's diagnoses, we may be dealing with intense anxiety of our own as we love someone who is so deeply hurting, and possibly in a self-destructive mode. In addition to anxiety, we may wrestle with guilt. Remember there are physiological elements at work here. Be kind to yourself. Be open. Professional guidance may be needed in managing such stress and anxiety.

We may wrestle with grief, as well. We must recognize that grief is a part of processing a life-altering diagnosis. We grieve loss. There is loss, and therefore deep sorrow, involved when a critical health condition is diagnosed. The path to health and strength involves accepting our circumstances and allowing ourselves to grieve. Acknowledge the heartbreak. We feel. We ache. We cry. Oh, do we cry.

Sometimes we find ourselves reeling with different and even conflicting emotions. This is completely normal, and it is okay. We are human! The experts say we should take a few moments each day (more often, if needed), to acknowledge and accept what we are feeling. (This is how we validate our own emotions.)

- Writing down your feelings can be healing and clarifying.

- Continue to counter anxiety and stress.

- Allow yourself to cry.

- Grieve. Grieve fully the losses and changes.

- Consider seeking professional help.

- Know that this takes time.

Wrestle with reality:

It can be very challenging to accept reality when a loved one is diagnosed with a serious psychological illness. Sometimes we might feel this explains some past behavior. Sometimes we just feel shock. Yet somehow we must come to a place of acceptance, and begin to deal with the facts, staying present with our situation. One of the most agonizing struggles for me was trying not to look back and compare to how things were just a short while ago. Ruminating nearly suffocated me. I continue to grapple with it, and wish I could supply some instant remedy, but along these lines I can only say you are not alone. This is incredibly hard. Yet, perhaps it may help you keep moving forward if you can remember:

- Denial only makes the pain worse.

- Grieve for what you've lost.

- Accept and deal with what you have.

Wrestle with your thought life:

Throbbing wounds drain and sap us. Sometimes it is hard to think. Surprisingly, a few seemingly small truths have proven to be especially soothing, supportive, and strengthening to me.

When facing difficult times, and when I've been hanging on by a thread, I find I have to simplify life to the core by asking myself: *What really matters? What is important here?* Sometimes this practice can help me regain focus and press on.

Often, I attempt to move forward by following advice I read decades ago from writer Elisabeth Elliot (I apologize, I do not recall which book), who taught me: *Do the next thing.* I may not be able to do what I really want to do (heal my hurting child), but what is facing me? What needs to be done right now? Maybe I need to do some helpful work for her, but maybe I need to make a sandwich, fold laundry, return a phone call, or buy soccer shoes for my son. Positive forward motion may be very small and incremental. It may seem unrelated or unimportant. It is not. It matters.

You are doing the best you can do.

As simple and overused as this may seem, there really is meaning and validity in the instruction: *Take it one day at a time.* It seems to be upheld by almost every religious and psychological counsel I've encountered. And in our worlds, where the manic can be so dangerous and the depression can be so deadly, it really becomes a healing remedy. We cannot predict tomorrow. We can only live today. And I'll be honest with you — in the times of deepest grief or crisis, I've had to take life one *minute* at a time … even one *breath* at a time … We can pursue professional help and medication and books and groups and take walks and scented bubble baths and pour out love and try our best, yet with all that, even if we could do absolutely everything, trying to live in the best way possible, we can only take it one day at a time. That's it.

Years ago, very early in this journey, the most healing words that ever came to me were spoken by a beloved counselor who grew to be more like family, and knew us well. She leaned in and tenderly said, *"You are doing the best you can do."* The power of those words is breathtaking. They have comforted and strengthened and carried me many a weary mile.

These measures build fortitude, sustaining us as we carry on with love and hope and kindness, which are universal needs and gifts.

Our hearts are big enough. We can do this.

- Ask: What really matters?

- Do the next thing.

- Take it one day at a time.

- Remind ourselves we are doing the best we can do.

Wrestle with deeper issues:

You may uncover unexpected interior pain and recognize you need to deal with some of your own concerns. The healthier and more whole you are, the more you can assist your loved one. Everyone deserves good health!

- Seek counseling.

- Consult a physician.

Wrestle with healthy living and creating balance:

Let's be honest … work, rest, and wrestling all require time and energy. We may find ourselves wrestling with the wrestling! Furthermore, we may be struggling with feeling limited or helpless. It's excruciating to watch someone we love hurt so much. It is exhausting, too. And while we're wrestling with so many thoughts and emotions, life still demands our attention: other children, spouses, jobs, aging parents, car repairs, unscrubbed toilets …

It might be worthwhile to assess your life, prioritize, and see what you can delegate. As difficult as this is for most of us, ask for help, especially during times of crisis. Reach out to family, your faith community, book club, bowling team, etc. So often people want to help, but they don't know what to do. Give them specific tasks. Allow them to provide meals if your child is in the hospital, or run errands for you while you rest, or babysit for younger children while you take your loved one to a counseling appointment.

Take a page from our prescription to our children, remembering that *our* good health is nourished by some of the same vital components. Try your best to take steps, great and small, that can keep you going.

- Tend to the basics: nutrition, sleep, exercise.

- Tend to anxiety and stress.

- Talk with a physician or counselor.

- Consider your household needs.

- Ask for help.

- Rest.

- Engage in small, pleasant activities, if possible.

- Seek the company of loving, caring, supportive people.

- Take advice from Dr. Ilardi's book.*

- Take life one day at a time.

- Remind yourself you are doing the best you can do.

*To further strengthen you in coping and dealing with anxiety and stress, read *The Depression Cure: The 6-Step Program to Beat Depression without Drugs* by Dr. Stephen Ilardi, Ph.D. Refer to Chapter Six for more information.

Wrestle with building your support team:

Balancing work and rest and wrestling and care and life and all that these tasks entail is an ongoing endeavor. We sincerely need the friendship of a few trusted people; however, in this situation, we may need more support — a safe place where we can share openly.

- Talk to others with similar experiences.

- Locate support groups.

- Seek counseling.

- Look to your faith community.

- Lean into your faith.

Resilience

The word *resilience* motivates me to persevere. Resilience is paramount to our coping and surviving, helping and thriving. We need resilience. We need to be able to bounce into action during crisis. We need to be able to spring to a response that instills health and life into our children's lives. We need to be able to absorb pain, feel our emotions, yet recover swiftly in order to carry on with our work of love and coaching life. We need energy for the sprint AND endurance for the distance.

We need energy for the sprint AND endurance for the distance.

We need to incorporate healthy coping habits into our lives. If we nourish ourselves with proper care and rest, and wrestle with issues and ways to strengthen ourselves and garner support, then we are doing what we can. We need to be able to encourage our hurting children, *and* encourage our hurting selves.

A core of our endurance and hope lies in this capacity to encourage ourselves as best we can. Even as we pour out love and positive messages to our children, we can also take notes from the coaching we offer to them — and strengthen our own hearts with the gifts of thankfulness, gratitude, inspiration, and faith. Take strength from the benefits of perspective and hope that accompany journaling. Keep a record of things that stir up thankfulness. Nurture a spirit of gratitude. Look for the beautiful and embrace it. Seek out sayings, positive readings, or spiritual texts that uplift. Pursue depth in faith. Hope, energy, and wisdom for the journey spring from a Power greater than us. Seek, find, and lean into the faith that heals.

Little steps can carry us many miles. As we endeavor to become more and more resilient, through experience, sheer will, optimism, or prayer, we will grow in strength and ability. And as we look for inspiration and intentionally cultivate an attitude of gratitude, we will grow in perseverance, hope, and courage.

Perhaps there is a cyclical nature to what we do … we respond, we pour ourselves out, we encourage, we breathe and rest and recover and try to regain strength and restore our hearts to continue doing the good work we need to do to love our hurting children and build up our families. We keep striving and hoping. We carry on in love. We do not give up. We continue to do the best we can do.

CHAPTER TEN

Review and Wrap-Up

Reflect

We are fighting for our children in a dark and painful arena.

Despite any troubling behaviors or difficult circumstances, and in spite of our own heartbreak, if we can remember that our children are in pain, then we can respond with compassion and patience. We pour into the relationships; we pour out love. Health and healing and hope begin here.

Review

Essentially:

- We need to know everything we can,

- be willing to do anything we can,

- know that we are doing all that we can,

- and believe we are doing the best that we can do.

I hope I have shown you:

- Some things you can do, immediately.

- Some things you can learn.

- Resources for further study.

- Thoughts for coping.

- Encouragement to continue on.

As a reminder, I hoped to create a piece that would provide excellent direction as briefly as possible to help parents who love and care for children in pain. Parents need resources, education, support, and connection. My wish has been to put forward an overview, not create overload. I never intended to overwhelm you with book titles! Yet, fueled by passion and a great desire to help, I have introduced you to the best I have found. With different experiences, personalities, explanations, expressions, and writing styles, the authors of the books recommended are in harmony in their compassionate tones that effectively guide us into speaking the language that our hurting children can hear.

Living life in pain is hard. In their pain, our children gasp and flail and grasp in vain at unhealthy options. In our pain, we gasp and flail and struggle as we strive to prevent self-harming, dangerous behaviors, and suicidal thoughts. Their actions so often beget more suffering. And we want our actions to make a positive difference. When it comes to suicide prevention, face the facts, summon up strength and courage, prepare for tough situations, emotional challenges, and hard conversations ... but do it. *Your child's life is at stake.*

We want to unite our hearts to theirs. Everything here reinforces my heart's cry as we endeavor to build up the relationships and touch the heart of their emotions first. Our words matter. Our hearts matter. We can communicate love and breed health through acceptance, compassion, validation, and coaching life.

That is the heartbeat of this message. This is how we can pump life-giving fuel into their souls. We keep loving and sharing and fighting the good fight and holding on to hope.

Renew

Although looking back can be painful, it can also stir compassion. Traveling back into memories stored deep in the heart, we can recall the day of a child's birth and ponder the sweet and precious moments of life, cherishing the strengths of our children and relishing the joys each child has brought. This is still that same little person we once held in our arms. Most of us never could have imagined how much pain someone we would love and raise could experience. We hurt with them, we suffer from feelings of helplessness, confusion, and more. But at the bottom of all these tragic feelings are the same hearts of love we've always had for our children.

So we start where we are. We breathe deeply. We seek strengthening measures.

Our children need us! We need to strengthen ourselves in order to help our babies. We need to be strong in body, mind, and spirit. Whether we need to add exercise, take vitamins, or seek counseling, we need to be at our healthiest to do our jobs well. As we strive to be better parents, we can learn how to shepherd our children through their emotions and assist them in their challenges while nurturing relationships that are rich and beautiful. We persevere with research, pursuing appropriate avenues of assistance available to us. We learn to speak the language that loves, lifts, and heals. We wrestle with issues and expand our capacity to bear up. And if life takes us down the hardest roads, we will have resources and support in place to help us cope as we keep loving our families, living life fully, and holding onto hope.

May you find strength, hope, peace, and healing.

– Kimberly Griffin

RESOURCES

Critical Connections:

Online References:

Helpguide – My current favorite, at www.helpguide.org, provides a clear, easy to use website full of countless amazing articles on almost every topic. Best of all, a lot of heart and unique insight is presented.

National Alliance on Mental Illness (NAMI) – A veritable powerhouse, their website, www.nami.org, is packed with information. We can look up symptoms, read about specific disorders, discover useful articles, educational opportunities, and find local contacts.

Depression and Bipolar Support Alliance (DBSA) – Another strong source of information and connection, their website address is www.dbsalliance.org.

Note: Both NAMI and DBSA facilitate local support groups.

National Institute of Mental Health (NIMH) – at www.nimh.nih.gov, is another long-standing, well-respected organization offering a wide range of information.

The Braveheart Connection – Our family hopes to encourage with an offering that is small scale but full of good intentions: www.thebraveheartconnection.com.

Also, explore Psychology Today, www.psychologytoday.com, or Psych Central, www.psychcentral.com. Columns by Dr. Karyn Hall include *Pieces of Mind* and *The Emotionally Sensitive Person*, respectively. (In Chapter Six I specifically mentioned Karyn Hall's article, "Understanding Validation: A Way to Communicate Acceptance," in her *Pieces of Mind* column at www.psychologytoday.com.)

Support Groups and Meaningful Connections:

In addition to NAMI and DBSA, many area religious organizations offer local support groups. Jewish Family Services are very proactive, as are many individual synagogues and churches, especially large ones. In most cases these groups are open to the community, whatever one's faith or beliefs. Begin by calling local organizations and asking questions.

Certain communities boast centers or clinics that treat specific disorders. Some of these centers hold classes for family members to learn skills like DBT. Sometimes classes for families are held at county mental health centers or in counseling offices. These may be difficult to find; the internet will be the best avenue for a search. Valerie Porr has developed numerous resources to help (www.tara4bpd.org), including classes and workshops (in New York City) to teach families principles from her book. I do not have experience with this, but trust the source based on her book. Recently, I have been looking into NAMI's free, twelve session course called Family-to-Family. It teaches families about mental illness, treatment, coping and communication strategies, and more, as it builds connections amongst families.

Finding even one other person who experiences and understands our challenges can provide immeasurable comfort and companionship. Connecting with others brings a fresh strength and promise.

BOOKS*

Alphabetized by title within categories.

The Essential Library:

The Depression Cure: The 6-Step Program to Beat Depression without Drugs by Dr. Stephen Ilardi, Ph.D. (Da Capo Press, a member of the Perseus Books Group, Cambridge, MA, 2009).

How I Stayed Alive When My Brain Was Trying to Kill Me: One Person's Guide to Suicide Prevention by Susan Rose Blauner (Quill, an imprint of HarperCollins Publishers, New York, NY 2002).

Loving Someone with Bipolar Disorder: Understanding and Helping Your Partner by Julie A. Fast and John D. Preston, Psy.D. (New Harbinger Publications, Inc., Oakland, CA, 2004).

Overcoming Borderline Personality Disorder: A Family Guide for Healing and Change by Valerie Porr, M.A. (Oxford University Press, Inc., New York, NY, 2010).

Validation Vitals:

Loving Someone with Borderline Personality Disorder: How to Keep Out-of-control Emotions from Destroying Your Relationship by Shari Y. Manning, Ph.D. (The Guilford Press, New York, NY, 2011).

Overcoming Borderline Personality Disorder: A Family Guide for Healing and Change by Valerie Porr, M.A. (Oxford University Press, Inc., New York, NY, 2010).

The Power of Validation: Arming Your Child Against Bullying, Peer Pressure, Addiction, Self-Harm & Out-of-Control Emotions by Karyn D. Hall, Ph.D. and Melissa H. Cook, LPC (New Harbinger Publications, Inc., Oakland, CA, 2012).

Manageable Psychology to Help Us Help Our Children:

The Dialectic Behavior Therapy Skills Workbook: Practical DBT Exercises for Learning Mindfulness, Interpersonal Effectiveness, Emotion Regulation & Distress Tolerance by Matthew McKay, Ph.D., Jeffrey C. Wood, Psy.D., Jeffrey Brantley, MD (New Harbinger Publishers, Inc., Oakland, CA, 2007).

Other Excellent Books on Mental Illness:

Bipolar Disorder Demystified: Mastering the Tightrope of Manic Depression by Lana R. Castle (Marlowe & Company, (an imprint of Avalon Publishing Group Incorporated, New York, NY, 2003).

Borderline Personality Disorder Demystified: An Essential Guide for Understanding and Living with BPD by Robert O. Friedel, MD, (Da Capo Press, a member of the Perseus Books Group, Cambridge, MA, 2004).

The Essential Family Guide to Borderline Personality Disorder: New Tools and Techniques to Stop Walking on Eggshells by Randi Kreger (Hazeldon, Center City, MN, 2008).

The Family Guide to Mental Health Care by Lloyd I. Sederer, MD (W.W. Norton & Company, New York, NY, 2013).

Helping Someone with Mental Illness — A Compassionate Guide for Family, Friends, and Caregivers by Rosalynn Carter with Susan K. Golant (Times Books, a division of Random House, New York, NY, 1998).

I Hate You Don't Leave Me: Understanding the Borderline Personality, by Jerold. J. Kreisman, MD, and Hal Straus (A Perigee Book, New York, NY, 2010).

Top Reads for Compassionate, Relational Parenting:

Between Parent and Child: The Best Selling Classic That Revolutionized Parent-Child Communication by Dr. Haim Ginott (Three Rivers Press, Random House Inc., New York, NY, orig. pub. 1965, revised and updated by Dr. Alice Ginott and Dr. H. Wallace Goddard, 2003).

The Power of Validation: Arming Your Child Against Bullying, Peer Pressure, Addiction, Self-Harm & Out-of-Control Emotions by Karyn D. Hall, Ph.D. and Melissa H. Cook, LPC (New Harbinger Publications, Inc., Oakland, CA, 2012).

Raising an Emotionally Intelligent Child By John Gottman, Ph.D., with Joan DeClaire (Simon & Schuster Paperbacks, New York, NY, 1997).

Extra Titles for Parents with Younger Children:

The Bipolar Child: The Definitive and Reassuring Guide to Childhood's Most Misunderstood Disorder by Demitri Papolos, MD and Janice Papolos (Three Rivers Press, New York, NY, 2007).

The Difficult Child by Stanley Tureki, MD, with Leslie Tonner (Bantam Books, New York, NY, 1985).

Not Specific to Mental Illness, but Supportive for Parenting Through Tough Times:

Sticking with Your Teen: How to Keep from Coming Unglued No Matter What by Joe White with Lissa Halls Johnson (Tyndale House Publications, Inc., Carol Stream, IL, 2006).

In a Class by Itself – Should be Read by Every Parent, Educator, and Human:

Emotional Intelligence by Daniel Goleman (Bantam Books, New York, NY, 1995).

Psychiatric Hospitalization Information and Support:

How to Cope When Your Loved One is in the Psychiatric Hospital by Kimberly Griffin (The Braveheart Connection, LLC, self-published via CreateSpace, Charleston, SC, 2016).

For Our Own Personal Strength, Support, Acceptance, and Coping:

Acceptance Therapy by Lisa Engelhardt, illustrated by R.W. Alley (One Caring Place, Abbey Press, St. Meinrad, IN, 1992).

The Chemistry of Joy Workbook: Overcoming Depression Using the Best of Brain Science, Nutrition, and the Psychology of Mindfulness by Henry Emmons, MD, Susan Bourgerie, MA, LP, Carolyn Denton, MA, LN, and Sandra Kacher, MSW, LICSW (New Harbinger Publishers, Inc., Oakland, CA, 2012).

The Depression Cure: The 6-Step Program to Beat Depression without Drugs by Dr. Stephen Ilardi, Ph.D. (Da Capo Press, a member of the Perseus Books Group, Cambridge, MA, 2009).

For Advocacy and Hope on a Broader Scale:

Within Our Reach: Ending the Mental Health Care Crisis by Rosalynn Carter with Susan K. Golant and Kathryn E. Cade (Rodale, Inc., New York, NY, 2010).

*The internet provides numerous additional resources. Also, most books offer lengthy book lists in an appendix. This list includes only those with which I have had personal and positive experience, and is not an exhaustive list of everything read or available.

SUICIDE PREVENTION

Hotlines:

Not just for the individuals considering suicide. We who love and care for them can also call for help and consultation.

1.800.273.TALK and 1.800.SUICIDE – National Suicide Prevention Lifelines.

Websites:

Suicide Prevention Lifeline
www.suicidepreventionlifeline.org
See article: http://www.suicidepreventionlifeline.org/learn/warningsigns.aspx

HelpGuide.org
www.helpguide.org
See article: http://www.helpguide.org/articles/suicide-prevention/suicide-prevention-helping-someone-who-is-suicidal.htm

National Alliance on Mental Illness (NAMI)
www.nami.org
See article: https://www.nami.org/Learn-More/Know-the-Warning-Signs

The National Foundation for Suicide Prevention
www.afsp.org
See article: www.afsp.org/preventing-suicide/suicide-warning-signs

National Institute of Mental Health (NIMH)
www.nimh.nih.gov
See article: http://www.nimh.nih.gov/health/topics/suicide-prevention/suicide-prevention-studies/warning-signs-of-suicide.shtml

Suicide.org
www.suicide.org
See article: http://www.suicide.org/suicide-warning-signs.html

Book:

How I Stayed Alive When My Brain Was Trying to Kill Me: One Person's Guide to Suicide Prevention by Susan Rose Blauner (Quill, an imprint of HarperCollins Publishers, New York, NY 2002).

ACKNOWLEDGMENTS

First, I wish to thank the tender hearts of my friends from the Shameless family ... for their delightful, generous spirits, and their willingness to share and help.

I am grateful to the authors of the books listed as Resources. I hold such high regard and appreciation for their works.

To Jen and Brenda for proofreading/editing help, kindness, support, and friendship beyond measure: there are no words to convey my love and appreciation.

Thanks to Julia, for her time, input, expertise, and what she has meant to us in helping our daughter.

I am deeply humbled by the encouragement of Ann and Bill, and so blessed by all the prayer time, friendship, and incredible support.

Love and hugs to all our extended family members and friends who have ached with us during the years of loss and pain. Hope rises.

Finally, and most importantly, I wish to thank my wonderful husband and my six beautiful children. Of course, I am immensely indebted to my daughter who struggles with these diagnoses. Without her willingness to be vulnerable and open in order to help others, this work would not have happened. She is fighting forward, and we are walking hand in hand. The power and strength of family uplifts and carries. Every single member of my family has offered some degree of help and support to me in pursuing several of these heart-wrenching, personal writing projects. But bigger than that, in life, we have lived through way too many painful and sorrowful challenges with passion, patience, endless love, and unending hope. May our futures be bright and joyful.

REFERENCES

Amygdala. (n.d.) In Wikipedia. Retrieved August 23, 2016 from http.//en.wikipedia/Amygdala.

"Brain Basics" (n.d.), National Institute of Mental Health. Retrieved August 23, 2016 from www.nimh.nih.gov.

Blauner, Susan Rose. *How I Stayed Alive When My Brain Was Trying to Kill Me: One Person's Guide to Suicide Prevention.* New York: Quill, an imprint of HarperCollins Publishers, 2002. Print.

Duckworth, Ken. "NAMI Honors Dr. Marsha Linehan, The Creator of Dialectical Behavior Therapy." *National Alliance on Mental Illness.* 5 October, 2015. Web. Originally published in NAMI's Fall 2015 *Advocate.* (www.nami.org)

"Emotion Regulation Circuit Weakened in Borderline Personality Disorder" (October 2, 2008), National Institute of Mental Health. Retrieved August 23, 2016 from www.nimh.nih.gov.

Fast, Julie A. and John D. Preston, Psy. D. *Loving Someone with Bipolar Disorder: Understanding and Helping Your Partner.* Oakland: New Harbinger Publications, Inc., 2004. Print.

Goleman, Daniel. *Emotional Intelligence.* New York: Bantam Books, 1995. Print.

Ginott, Dr. Haim. G. *Between Parent and Child: The Bestselling Classic that Revolutionized Parent-Child Communication.* Revised and Updated by Dr. Alice Ginott and Dr. H. Wallace Goddard. New York: Three Rivers Press, a member of the Crown Publishing Group, a division of Random House, Inc., 2003. Print.

Hall, Karyn D., Ph.D., and Melissa H. Cook, LPC. *The Power of Validation. Arming Your Child Against Bullying, Peer Pressure, Addiction, Self-Harm & Out-of-Control Emotions.* Oakland: New Harbinger Publications, Inc., 2012. Print.

Manning, Shari Y., Ph.D. *Loving Someone with Borderline Personality Disorder: How to Keep Out-of-control Emotions from Destroying Your Relationship.* New York: The Guilford Press, 2011. Print.

McKay, Matthew, Ph.D., Jeffrey C. Wood, Psy.D., and Jeffrey Brantley, MD. *The Dialectic Behavior Therapy Skills Workbook: Practical DBT Exercises for Learning Mindfulness, Interpersonal Effectiveness, Emotion Regulation & Distress Tolerance.* Oakland: New Harbinger Publishers, Inc., 2007. Print.

Porr, Valerie. *Overcoming Borderline Personality Disorder: A Family Guide for Healing and Change.* New York: Oxford University Press, Inc., 2010. Print.